QUILT AS YOU GO ▼

'The world always
seems brighter when
you've just made
something that
wasn't there before'.
Neil Gaiman

QUILT AS YOU GO ▶▶

CAROLYN FORSTER

A practical guide to
14 inspiring techniques & projects

FAVOURITE FLOWER POEMS

ROMANTIC MODERNS
English Writers, Artists and the Imagination
from Virginia Woolf to John Piper
ALEXANDRA HARRIS

SEARCH PRESS

First published in 2022

Search Press Limited
Wellwood, North Farm Road,
Tunbridge Wells, Kent TN2 3DR

Text copyright © Carolyn Forster 2022

Photographs by Mark Davison
Styling by Lisa Brown
Photographs and design copyright
© Search Press Ltd. 2022

ISBN: 978-1-78221-940-8
ebook ISBN: 978-1-78126-934-3

The Publishers and author can accept no responsibility for
any consequences arising from the information, advice or
instructions given in this publication.

Suppliers
For details of suppliers, please visit the Search Press website:
www.searchpress.com

Extra copies of the templates are available from
www.bookmarkedhub.com.

The projects in this book have been made using imperial
measurements, and the metric equivalents provided have
been calculated following standard conversion practices.
The metric measurements are often rounded to the nearest
0.25cm for ease of use except in rare circumstances;
however, if you need more exact measurements, there
are a number of excellent online converters that you can
use. Always use either metric or imperial measurements,
not a combination of both.

Publisher's note
All the step-by-step photographs in this book feature the
author, Carolyn Forster.

Acknowledgements

With grateful thanks to the ever-
wonderful team at Search Press who
again have made sense of my vision
for this book.

I would like to thank my students who
always continue to inspire me to be a
better teacher.

A big thank you to my friends who
happily participated in the Potholder
Quilt on page 70. When there was a
lot going on in the world, they used
their precious sewing time to do this.
I am forever grateful.

And I would like to name and
acknowledge Becky Robbins for the
support and professionalism she has
continued to pour into our working
relationship over the many books we
have produced together: thank you.

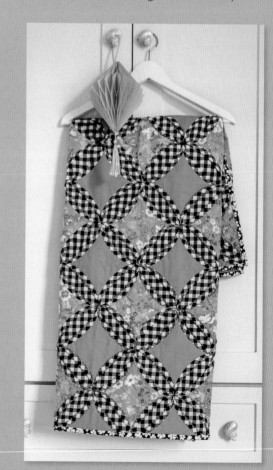

CONTENTS

TECHNIQUES

INTRODUCTION

One of the most popular classes that I teach is a Quilt As You Go (QAYG) class. We cover one technique, and the method comes as a revelation to many people. You can make whole and sometimes huge quilts, quilted in sections as you make the blocks, then put them together almost seamlessly, but definitely painlessly. No more trying to lay out and tack/baste a quilt on the floor, no more sitting under a pile of fabric every time you want to quilt, or trying to push the cumbersome heap under the sewing-machine needle.

Interestingly, when I speak to people about QAYG, they often tell me that they have tried it, but it didn't work for them. I ask which method they used, and am often told that there is only one. It comes as an eye-opener to many that there are numerous ways to quilt as you go, to make and quilt a quilt, either by hand or machine, that makes it manageable and portable. I've tried lots of QAYG methods and I pick and choose to make sure I work with the one most appropriate for the quilt at hand, or where and how I want to work.

But finding out about all of the different ways to quilt as you go is time-consuming – there are bits in books and magazines, but no book with them all in. So by putting together all of the methods that I can find and have tried (and there may be some yet to be discovered), I'm helping you as much as I'm helping myself. Think of the old adage, 'How do you eat an elephant? One bite at a time'. Now think of making a quilt. If you've found the sheer size and scale of the process of quiltmaking somewhat daunting in the past, there will be a QAYG solution for you.

So what exactly is QAYG?

Very simply put, it is the act of piecing and quilting simultaneously with the aim of making the process manageable and often portable. It is the method of stitching patchwork so that you are creating the quilted texture at the same time as sewing the patches to backing and wadding/batting. It can also take other forms (for example, I have included Suffolk puffs, see page 126), but the bottom line is that in the act of making the patchwork you are also making the quilting or the look of quilting.

Why would I want to try QAYG?

If you struggle with the tacking/basting of a whole quilt, either through lack of space, or because you don't have the desire or ability to crawl around on the floor, then making a quilt in small, manageable sections is often the answer. It also makes the work portable, and something that you can do in small spaces of time. If you want a super-speedy machine-stitched-in-a-day type of quilt, there is also a method for that. You have the flexibility to create, because there are methods to suit your needs.

Where would I want to do QAYG?

If you like to take some sewing with you to meet up with friends, or to travel and stitch on holiday, or to fill in time in waiting rooms, then there will be a hand technique for you. It means that leaving the house, or the country, does not mean you have to leave your quilting behind.

When would I want to do QAYG?

I still make many quilts in the traditional way: piecing the top, layering with wadding/batting and backing, tacking/basting, and then quilting a whole big quilt. Some quilts need that, and that is great, but it's nice to have the option of a different way of working, too: envelope quilts quilted on planes and trains... Siddi quilts (see page 100) meditatively stitched while listening to the radio. There is really no limit to using these techniques, which means that you can be stitching and making a quilt any time and anywhere you want.

How do I QAYG?

In this book I have put together 14 different methods to whet your appetite. For each there is a step-by-step walk-through of the technique to get you started and then a project to try it out.

Which QAYG method is right for me?

Depending on how you want to work, there will be a technique that will enable you to do so in manageable and often portable fashion.

Hand stitching:
▶ Quilting on the go: hand-pieced blocks, hand-quilted (see page 26)
▶ Manx log cabin: hand-pieced (see page 60)
▶ Potholder quilting: hand-pieced blocks, hand-quilted (see page 70)
▶ Japanese reversible quilting: hand-pieced, quilted and joined (see page 78)
▶ Envelope quilting: hand-pieced, quilted and joined (see page 86)
▶ Cathedral windows (see page 92)
▶ Siddi quilting (see page 100)
▶ Suffolk puffs (see page 126)
▶ Pojabi patchworking (see page 132)

Machine stitching:
▶ Machine joining front and back (see pages 40 and 48)
▶ Stitch-and-flip blocks, machine-quilted (see page 36)
▶ Piecemaker's quilting: machine-quilted (see page 52)
▶ Appliqué quilting: machine-joined front and back (see page 108)
▶ Lined circles: machine-quilted (see page 114)
▶ Fringed quilting (see page 120)
▶ Pojabi patchworking (see page 132)

Hand and machine stitching:
▶ Quilting on the go: machine-pieced, hand-quilted (see page 26)
▶ Machine-joined front, hand-finished back (see page 30)
▶ Stitch-and-flip blocks, hand-quilted (see page 36)
▶ Piecemaker's quilting: hand-quilted (see page 52)
▶ Manx log cabin (see page 60)
▶ Potholder quilting (see page 70)
▶ Envelope quilting: hand- or machine-quilted (see page 86)
▶ Cathedral windows (see page 92)
▶ Lined circles: hand quilted (see page 114)
▶ Pojabi patchworking (see page 132)

What can I make using QAYG?

The first things that come to mind are quilts. Quilts of all sizes can utilize these methods. For example, stitch-and-flip can be sewn with or without wadding/batting, making lightweight coverlets for the warm weather. Pojabi, Manx log cabin, Suffolk puffs and cathedral windows quilts all make light throws with no wadding/batting, which you can use whatever the season. Picnic quilts and baby quilts, table runners and Christmas stockings, and bags and storage containers can all be made taking advantage of the methods here. Use this book as a stepping stone into each method and then explore in more depth as time and your creativity allows.

HISTORY ▶▶

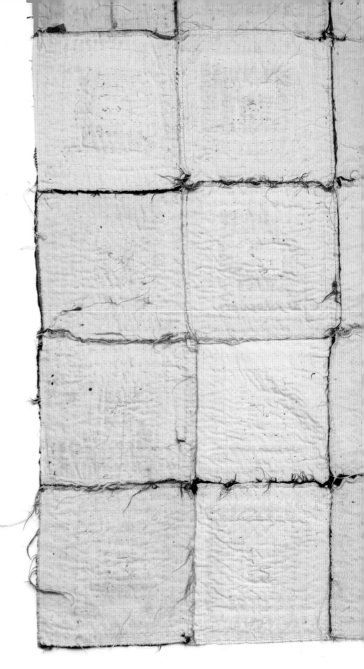

Quilting as you go is not a new technique. Stitchers and quilt makers have been thinking up ways to help them make their quilt-making manageable, portable and accessible for many years, possibly many more than you would guess.

One type of quilting, known as potholder quilting, has been around since at least 1856, with a wonderful example seen in the American Museum of Folk Art, New York, USA. It is characterized by patchwork blocks being stitched, quilted, often signed and bound before being sewn together to make one whole quilt. I have included an example of this stye of quilting on pages 70-77.

The quilts were sometimes friendship or presentation quilts, but a large number documented were made during the US Civil War (12th April 1861–9th April 1865). These were made by women to help raise funds or to donate to hospitals for the injured soldiers. They are a great example of a QAYG and friendship quilt all in one. The name is thought to have come from the custom of quilting and binding squares of fabric and wadding/batting to make an insulated pad to hold the handle of a pot, kettle or casserole, hence 'pot holder'.

It is not always easy to see or find historic examples of QAYG quilts, as often the construction method is not highlighted in documentation. The museum quilt mentioned above made no mention of it, and quilts that I have purchased over the years have all been identified by guess work; I have worked out their construction by peering at photographs and then asking questions.

The log cabin quilt (shown from the back, above right, and from the front, opposite), uses one of the blocks most associated with QAYG and the stitch-and-flip method. This quilt has no backing, and the blocks are stitched in a variety of heavy-weight fabrics onto a strong cotton fabric. Each block has then had some embroidery added in the centre of each block. Without testing some of the fabrics for composition it has been hard to date this one, but the seller did know that it had been owned and probably made by a lady between 1874 and 1961. The blocks were hand pieced and then machined together.

Another example of a well-known QAYG technique is the envelope or pocket quilting technique on pages 86–91; images of similar work can be found from the 1930s. If we look abroad to quilt-makers in Japan (folded reversible patchwork, see pages 78–85),

Korea (the Pojabi technique, see pages 132–139) and India (the Siddi quilting technique, see page 100–107), we can see many examples of quilt making where the process has been streamlined for manageability.

I think it is important to take onboard the historical significance of QAYG techniques, while also putting quilts into the context of quilters today, who may be looking for ways to make things easier.

▶ 1800s crib coverlet

The blocks (shown from the front, below left, and from the back, below right) seem to have had the design appliquéd onto squares of cotton bags (based on the printing seen on them), with a hem turned to the wrong side and the first row of appliqué on the block holding that hem in place.

Each block is then stitched and finished, then oversewn to hold the blocks together. There is no wadding/batting in this coverlet.

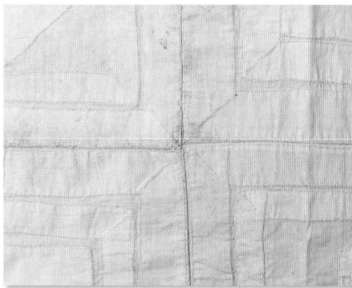

▶ Early 1900s coverlet

Another example, possibly from the early 1900s, is this blue and white quilt, technically a coverlet, as there is no wadding/batting. The back is shown below left; the front is shown below right.

The blocks have been well planned, with enough fabric purchased to complete the top in the two colours. The blocks are quite accurately stitched by hand, with most of the pattern matching up. The blocks seem to have been stitched together, and then a strip to cover the pressed-open seam added afterwards.

The binding on this has also been hand stitched. Looking at this it is possible to imagine the person sewing these blocks in their spare time, gradually building up enough to put a row together, then a full quilt, just as we would now. It is interesting to be able to look at these old quilts, and in some cases make one ourselves, replicating the method to get a greater understanding of the QAYG process.

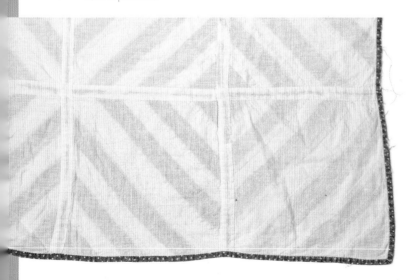

▶ 1930s log cabin coverlet

This log cabin coverlet is one that I have tried to re-create, as I was interested in how the blocks were put together with a type of flat-felled seam (see below and below right).

The blocks are stitched by hand, put together on the machine, and the border added by machine, with the same stitch-and-flip method as is used in the blocks. It also has a machine-finished binding. This is a nice example of blocks that were made to be portable and sewn by hand, and then stitched together when the maker had access to a sewing machine.

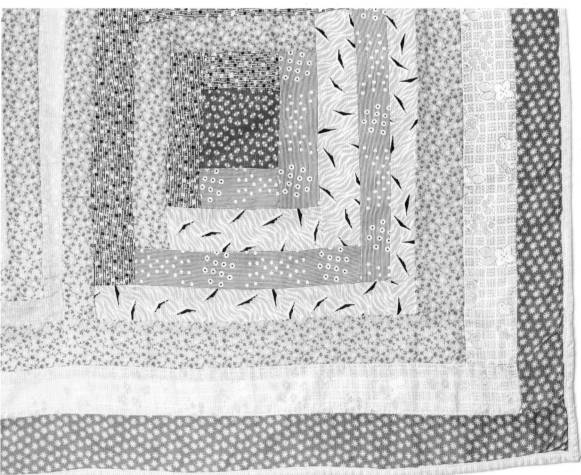

YOU WILL NEED ▶▶

FABRICS

As with all patchwork projects, if you can pre-wash fabrics
before using them then you lessen the likelihood of colour
run and shrinkage. If you can't do this (some pre-cuts make it
impractical), then add a dye-catching laundry sheet when you
wash your finished quilt. This will help to capture any loose
colour and stop it bleeding into other fabrics.

For the quilts in the book I've used a selection of different fabric types, as
the broad range of different techniques covered requires a range of different
fabrics. The usual patchwork-weight cottons work well for most of the quilting
techniques, but sometimes it is worth experimenting. For the Suffolk puffs (see
page 126), I used double gauze, while the Pojabi (see page 132) included
lightweight bark cloth and cotton-linen blends. The Japanese reversible
patchwork (see page 78) included old embroidered linens, while the Manx
log cabin (see page 60) was stitched on a backing of cotton damask. The
back of my Siddi quilt (page 100) was a cotton tea towel. The main thing
with the fabric choice is that it should be easy for you to work with and not
present problems. If you cannot stitch it, or it frays everywhere, then it is best
to look for a replacement.

　For some of the techniques you may want to use 'busy print' fabrics for the
backs of the blocks so that the seams don't show so much. For this, choose a
non-directional multicoloured print to really hide seams and sewing lines.

　For some techniques, if you find that colour shows through when a lighter
fabric is stitched over a darker fabric, keep some oddments of white fabric to
hand. You can slot this in under the lighter fabric, or, if you have the time, cut
back the darker fabric seam allowance (SA) so it is under the lighter fabric.

THREADS

There are many makes and types on the market, but this
list contains the threads I use most frequently in my sewing.
As with all things, try them out and see what you think –
nothing is written in stone.

▸ 50wt: for general machine-sewing and for hand appliqué.
▸ 40wt: for hand-finishing a binding and for machining if you need
　something slightly stronger or bolder.
▸ 28wt: for hand-piecing, machine-quilting, and fine hand-quilting.
▸ 12wt: for big stitch hand-quilting (see page 19).

NEEDLES

Generally these are the hand and machine needles that I use most often. You don't need many types, but I find that buying good-quality ones does make a difference. Again, if something works for you and you are getting the results that you want, keep on using what you use. But if you are feeling that the results could be better, or easier to work, then try something different.

Hand stitching:

‣ Betweens, no.6 for big stitch quilting; no.10 for fine hand quilting.
‣ Embroidery no.6 for big stitch quilting.
‣ Sharps nos.10 or 11 for hand piecing and hand finishing bindings.

Threading a needle

When threading a needle, I always find it easier to hold the thread and put the needle over it, rather than trying to poke the thread through the needle's eye. If you find threading the needle difficult, invest in a needle threader, or easy-thread needles.

Machine stitching:

‣ Sizes 70/10, 80/12 and 90/14 needles for general machine-pieced patchwork.
‣ Jeans, topstitch and quilting needles, especially for stitch-and-flip and the machine-joining techniques. You generally need a needle that is strong and makes a hole large enough to pull a thicker thread through. When you look closely, these needles will have a groove running down the shaft, which helps take the thread through the fabric.

SEWING MACHINE

You do not need a fancy sewing machine – as long as it does a straight stitch you can quilt as you go. You'll find lots of hints and tips in the instruction manual that comes with your machine, as well as troubleshooting pages.

Many machines can stitch through multiple layers without you needing to adjust the foot pressure on the top of the machine; others need a walking foot attached. Some sewing-machine brands have a walking foot built in, and if you are considering making many more quilts using the stitch-and-flip technique, machine-joining methods or the machine-completed binding, you may want to consider investing in one of those brands.

A large extension table is particularly useful when working with your machine. It will allow you to keep your work flat and gives you a better surface area in order to handle and control what you are working on. If your machine does not come with one, it is worth the investment, and it can be easily removed and folded away when not in use.

Housekeeping on your machine is very important when you are regularly stitching through multiple layers including wadding/batting. This sort of stitching generates a lot of lint, and this is often hidden under the foot plate and around the bobbin casing. If you can, give the area a little dust with a fine brush each time you change the bobbin. At other times, take the machine apart in the bobbin area following your instruction manual, and give it a proper clean. This will increase the working life of the machine and make your quilting a much better experience.

You will find certain feet useful:

‣ A ¼in (5mm) piecing foot with no guide is good for piecing patchwork.
‣ An in-the-ditch quilting foot is useful for stitching right in that ditch.
‣ A walking or even-feed foot is ideal for stitching through multiple layers of fabric.

WADDING/BATTING

The wadding/batting that you choose for these projects can make your life and the stitching process so much easier.

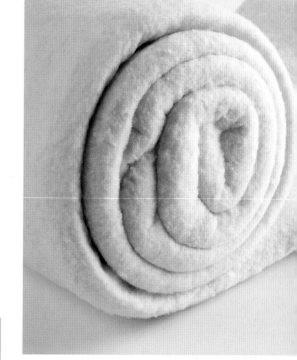

I either use a cotton and polyester blend (80/20) or a pure cotton wadding/batting. For many of the techniques shown here, the use of either of these waddings/battings will mean that the layers of the quilt will hold together, and not slip or shift. If you are really concerned that the layers may shift as you are working on them, use a spray baste on the backing fabric to adhere it to the wadding/batting.

Wadding/batting and backing fabrics are usually cut larger than the finished block size for many of the methods, especially quilting on the go (see page 26), and the stitch-and-flip way of working (see page 36). This is to allow for fabric movement and take up, which can occur when you stitch through multiple layers. When the block is complete, any extra wadding/batting and fabric is trimmed away as the block is squared up.

Tip

To increase the longevity of your equipment, especially scissors and rotary cutters, it is worth keeping dedicated items for cutting wadding/batting and quilt layers. The wadding/batting can dull the cutting blades, so if you want to keep equipment sharp, don't cut the wadding/batting with your favourite fabric scissors.

Joining wadding/batting pieces

Many of the methods in the book use small pieces of wadding/batting. The quilts are excellent for using up off-cuts in small blocks, and larger pieces of wadding/batting can be created from the scraps.

Use fusible fabric tape such as HeatnBond to join pieces of wadding/batting together.

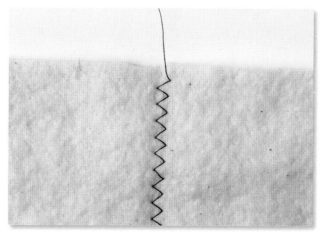

Or use a zigzag stitch on the sewing machine; butt the edges together and sew along the join to make larger pieces when needed. Use matching thread.

TOOLS

Cutting equipment

Scissors
Use a large pair of long-bladed scissors for cutting the fabrics. I have a specialist pair of quilting scissors that is ideal for this purpose. You will also want small scissors with fine points, which make snipping threads easy and give you more control over the blades.

Quick-unpick
Use this tool to undo sewing mistakes quickly and easily. I also use the point to help guide in the fabric under the machine foot, close to the needle, which helps to protect my fingers.

Rulers
Various specialist acrylic rulers are available that work with a rotary cutter and self-healing cutting mat to cut the fabric easily and quickly in layers where necessary. The various types that you could use for the projects in this book are given with the relevant project instructions.

Rotary cutter

Looking much like a pizza wheel, a rotary cutter cuts through up to about eight layers of fabric at a time. Keep the blade sharp and free of nicks, and cut through as many or as few layers as you are comfortable with.

Self-healing cutting mat

This is a purpose-made mat, available from craft stores, on which to cut your fabric using the rulers and cutters. It is marked into a grid that you can use to help you measure and cut the fabric in straight lines. Buy the largest size you can afford, as the larger the cutting mat, the less you will need to fold your fabric.

Other key equipment

Pins

Long, fine pins with a glass head are the most useful for keeping fabrics in place before stitching. However, sometimes short appliqué pins are also helpful, especially when hand piecing.

Fabric clips

These are especially useful when stitching several layers of fabric together, as when adding binding (see page 25) or joining blocks together (see page 42).

Quilter's tape measure

This type of tape measure is longer than a normal tape measure and so is useful for measuring bed lengths and quilt sides. It is 120in (300cm) long.

Template plastic

This is a sturdy but thin plastic that can be drawn on or traced through and then cut with normal scissors. To write on the plastic, you should use a fine permanent marker pen.

Iron

Your patchwork will need pressing, so a good hot iron is useful. You can use a steam iron, but be careful not to distort the seams when pressing.

Hera marker

This is a useful tool for creasing seams and marking quilting designs.

Chalk marker

This marker is used like a pen and leaves a thin white line on the fabric that brushes off easily. It is ideal for marking on patterns and stitch lines.

Quilting equipment

Thimbles

When I quilt I use a thimble with a ridge around its top on the finger which is underneath the work; I find that the ridge helps me make the stitches as I push the needle against it. On the hand above the work I wear a metal dimpled thimble to push the needle along. There are lots of thimbles and finger protectors to try, and it may take a while, and some patience, to find the ones that best work for you.

Although I try to use a combination of needle and thread that are smooth to work with, occasionally I find I need an extra tug to get the thread through the layers. Try using a needle grabber, or the side of a silicone thimble, to add extra grip.

Quilting needles

Also known as betweens, these are usually short needles with a round eye. They are available in a range of sizes to accommodate different threads and skill levels. If you are a beginner I suggest you start with a size 8 and aim to work up to using a 10 or 11, which are smaller. Generally, the smaller the needle the smaller the stitch you make, but this also depends on experience and the particular combination of fabrics and wadding/batting you are using. As a rule, use the needle size that is most comfortable in your hand.

For machine quilting you will usually need to change the needle in your sewing machine from a general sewing needle to a 'jeans' or machine quilting needle. Practice and knowledge of your machine will help you work out which is best.

Quilting thread

Quilting thread is slightly thicker than general sewing thread and forms the quilting stitches that hold the three layers of a quilt together. The reels that you buy will state whether they are for hand or machine quilting (sometimes they will work well for both).

Choose a colour that blends with the overall appearance of the quilt, unless you want the stitches to stand out on particular areas. Remember that for hand quilting, the thread will be visible as small stitches, but for machine quilting you will see a continuous line of thread on the front and back of the quilt.

Tacking/basting thread

Use a specialist thread for hand tacking/basting, as it can be broken easily and is cheaper than regular sewing thread, but holds the layers together securely for quilting.

Quilt hoop

Traditionally, you would use a quilting hoop for hand quilting large quilts, to make the process easier. However, for QAYG I don't usually find the need for one. Most of what I quilt is in small manageable pieces, and doesn't need a hoop. Once the project gets bigger, you may find using a hoop helps to keep the work flat, but generally one is not needed.

QUILTING ▶▶

MACHINE QUILTING

The running stitch that holds the three layers together can be stitched on the sewing machine. To make it easier to work, the quilt may need to be on a table that supports both the machine and the quilt without the quilt dragging. Generally, the machine will need to be fitted with a quilting or 'jeans' needle and a specialist machine-quilting thread should be used. Your usual supplier will be able to advise you on what to select, and it is always good to try different makes of thread to see which works best for you.

Free-motion quilting

This method of quilting on the machine allows you to move the stitches in any direction over the quilt and to make the stitches any length. This will usually involve dropping the feed dogs and using an open-toe darning foot, but check the manual for your particular sewing machine. Designs that are worked in this way include vermicelli quilting (see right). This is an all-over quilting design that can be worked by machine over any patchwork pattern. The free-motion design is worked on the machine with the feed dogs lowered and an open-toe darning foot in place. The pattern is self-guided and you can control the density of stitching yourself.

Straight-line quilting

For this method of machine quilting, the stitch length is set by you on the machine. You may find it easier to use an even-feed (walking) foot as it helps all the layers work through at the same pace and prevents dragging. This foot can also be used when you bind the quilt for the same reason. Diagonal lines are a popular choice (see below) but you can also work in vertical and/or horizontal lines or try echo quilting, where you repeat the outlines of the pieced shapes, a short but regular distance from the seams.

Vermicelli quilting.

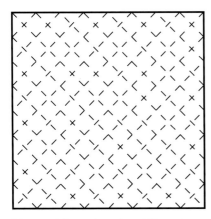

Diagonal lines placed at 45° angles.

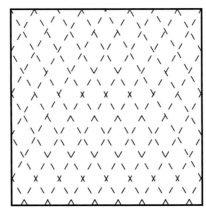

Diagonal lines placed at 60° angles.

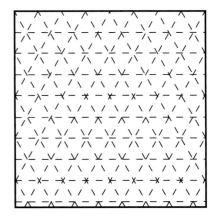

Diagonal lines placed at 60° angles with horizontal lines creating equilateral triangles.

HAND QUILTING

Starting the stitch

1 Start by cutting a length of thread as long as your arm. Tie a knot in the end you just cut. Thread the free end into the needle. You need to insert the needle down through the top layer of fabric and wadding/batting only to come up where you want to start, pulling on the thread so that the knot is embedded in the wadding/batting and the embedded thread will be quilted over, adding an extra layer of security for the thread.

2 If the knot won't pull through the fabric, use the point of the needle to poke the weave of the fabric to expand the hole where the knot needs to go through. Gently pull the thread until the knot goes into the wadding/batting and then, using the needle, push the threads back in place. Now you are ready to stitch.

BIG STITCH TIPS

This style of quilting uses a relatively thick thread and big stitches. The stitch length is often longer on the top surface of the quilt and smaller on the bottom. Big stitch quilting is a bold style of quilting and the designs are usually fairly widely spaced, therefore needing fewer lines, and taking less time to quilt.

- Follow the sequence on starting the stitch (left), and continue on. As you make the stitches, try to work with a rhythm to create even but large stitches that go through all three layers.

- I keep the needle hand still with the needle horizontal and move the finger that is on the underside of the quilt to create the stitches. Try different motions to see which is comfortable for you and creates the even stitches you want.

- I find it helpful to have a thimble on the middle finger of the needle hand for pushing the needle through, and a ridged thimble on the index finger of the hand under the quilt. The finger under the quilt pushes the layers up, creating a little 'hill' with the ridge of the thimble, which the needle is pushed against to make the stitch.

- When you have about 6in (15cm) of thread left in the needle, finish off and then start a new length of thread.

Stopping the stitch

At the end of the stitching, or if the thread is running out, you will need to finish off securely. Make sure you leave enough thread to enable you to do this - about 5–6in (15cm). It may seem a lot, but if you leave less than this, the process will be really fiddly.

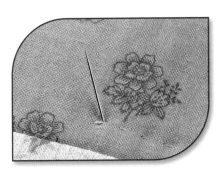 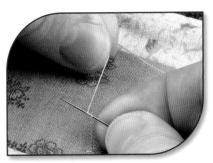 

1 Make the last stitch, going all the way through to the back of the quilt with the needle, then bring the needle back up at the beginning of the last stitch.

2 Pull the thread through and wrap it around the needle two or three times (it will depend on how thick your thread is and how densely woven the fabric is; you are making a knot that will pull through easily).

3 Put the needle into the middle of the last stitch, just underneath it, going through the front fabric and wadding/batting, travelling a needle's length away from the stitching. As you pull the thread, a knot will form that needs to be gently pulled through to embed in the wadding/batting. If the knot has a loop, smooth it out with your fingers before pulling it through. Snip the thread tail close to the quilt top.

BINDING ▶▶

Once the quilt is quilted, remove any tacking/basting stitches or pins. It is now ready for binding. First, I will show you how to bind your quilt with mitred corners. You need to start by joining fabric strips together to make a continuous length that goes all the way around your quilt. Use a strip width of 2½in (6.5cm).

JOINING STRIPS TOGETHER

I use a bias join for joining strips together, which results in less bulk when the fabric is folded over and wrapped around the edge of the quilt.

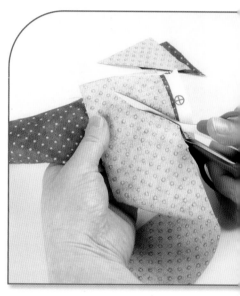

1 Take a fabric strip and lay a second fabric strip at 90 degrees on top of it, right sides facing. Allow an extra ⅜in (1cm) of fabric along each short edge, as shown. Stitch across the diagonal.

2 Join subsequent strips using chain piecing. To do this, open out the first two strips and lay a third strip face down on the end of the second strip, as in step 1. Stitch across the diagonal. Continue to add fabric strips until you have a piece that is long enough to go all round the quilt.

3 Cut through the joining threads and trim off the excess fabric at each join, leaving a ¼in (5mm) seam allowance. Press all the seams open neatly. You can now press your binding in half, long edges together and right sides out.

MOCK BIAS JOIN

Follow these steps to prepare the end of your binding for continuous mitred binding.

1 Press the binding in half, wrong sides together, if you have not already done so. Pull down one end at 90 degrees, as shown. Press at the folds.

2 Trim off the excess fabric at the end of the strip, leaving a ¼in (5mm) seam allowance.

CONTINUOUS MITRED BINDING

This type of binding has a mock bias join to complete the two ends.
Start by fitting an even-feed (walking) foot to your sewing machine and
prepare the binding end as explained for a mock bias join, opposite.

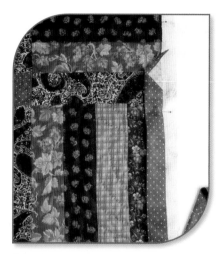

1 Lay the binding along one side of the quilt, raw edges aligned, and starting about one-third of the way along. Pin it in place. I do not usually trim the wadding/batting and backing to match the quilt front until the first steps of the binding are complete, but if you want to trim them now, you can do so.

2 Using the width of the even-feed (walking) foot to gauge the seam width, start stitching about 4in (10cm) away from the end of the binding. Sew down towards the corner, stopping about ½in (1cm) away from the edge. Secure the stitches.

3 Remove the quilt from under the machine and fold the binding at 90 degrees away from the quilt so that it lies in a straight line, aligned with the next raw edge.

4 Fold the binding back down onto the quilt, aligning the raw edges and creating a fold at the corner.

5 Start sewing at the folded edge and secure the stitches. Sew down to the next corner and repeat. Turn all the corners in the same way.

6 When you get to the last side, stitch towards the join and stop about 6in (15cm) away from it. Trim the binding at an angle so that it overlaps the start by about ½in (1cm).

7 Tuck the end into the start of the binding, as shown.

8 Continue stitching along the binding to secure the two ends.

9 Remove the quilt from the sewing machine. Trim away the wadding/ batting and backing fabric, if you haven't already.

10 Turn the binding over to the back of the quilt and pin it in place so that the folded edge meets up with the machine-stitched line.

11 When all the sides are pinned, fold each corner so that the bulk of the fabric lies under the fold and pin it in place.

12 Using slipstitch and a thread to match the binding, sew the binding to the backing fabric. Do not sew through to the front of the quilt, and hide the travelling stitches in the wadding/batting. When you reach the join, stitch along it.

13 Stitch the join round to the front of the fabric, then take the needle through to the back of the quilt and continue along.

14 As you reach each of the mitred corners, stitch them closed.

SQUARE-CORNERED BINDING

This is a simple basic binding to use when you want to add some colour and strength to the edge of your quilt. This version is sewn on the machine and finished by hand. Begin by cutting strips of binding 2½in (6.5cm) wide and join them with a crossway join so that you have four strips about 2in (5cm) longer than each side of the quilt. Press them in half lengthways, wrong sides together.

1 Sew one strip to the side of the quilt, matching the raw edges and using the width of the walking foot as your seam allowance. When you reach the end, trim the binding to line up with the top fabric, if necessary. Repeat this process on the opposite side of the quilt.

2 Trim off the surplus backing and wadding/batting in line with the raw edge of the binding. Finger press the binding away from the quilt top.

3 Repeat on the remaining sides of the quilt, aligning the raw edges of each strip with the raw edges of the binding strips already attached.

4 At the corners, trim away the surplus fabric and wadding/batting to make turning the binding in easier.

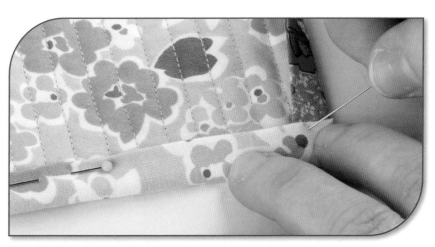

5 Fold the binding over onto the back of the quilt and pin it in place. Fold the corners so that the raw edges are concealed. Slipstitch the folded edge down, sewing along the open edges at the corners.

MITRED BINDING, MACHINE-FINISHED, **VERSION 1**

Finishing the quilt with binding often entails some hand-sewing. If you want to continue to make your quilt entirely on the machine, then try one of these two binding methods. This first method secures the binding from the front of the quilt, by sewing in the ditch of the binding seam. On the back there will be a visible line of stitching along the folded edge of the binding. For the second method, see opposite.

1 Cut enough 2½in (6.5cm) wide binding strips to go all the way around the quilt with 6in (15cm) added for an overlap to finish. Prepare as usual (see page 20).

2 Start by stitching the binding to the front of the quilt using a ¼in (5mm) seam allowance. Refer to page 21 for sewing around the corners.

3 Now turn the binding over to the back of the quilt. It will be wide enough to overlap the stitching line.

4 Use long pins to hold the binding in place, and secure the mitred corners as usual.

5 Now, from the front of the quilt, stitch in the ditch of the binding seam. You can usually feel the binding on the back, to ensure that you are sewing that in place at the same time, but the pins will keep it secure without distorting the binding.

6 At each corner, stop with the needle in the work, and lift the presser foot to turn the quilt before continuing along the next side. Finish by overlapping the stitches by 1in (2.5cm) and secure the threads.

7 On the front, the line of stitching is hidden in the ditch of the binding seam (7a), and on the back you will see a stitching line along the folded edge of the binding (7b).

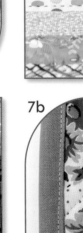

MITRED BINDING, MACHINE-FINISHED, **VERSION 2**

For this method, you will first stitch the binding onto the quilt from the back. To finish the binding, it is topstitched along the folded edge on the front of the quilt.

1 Cut and prepare the binding as usual. Stitch the binding to the quilt from the back using a ¼in (5mm) seam allowance. Refer to page 21 for sewing around the corners.

2 Turn the binding over to the front of the quilt. It will overlap the stitching line on the front. Secure it in place with fabric clips, making sure the mitred corners are neat and secure.

3 Start stitching on the folded edge of the binding, which is on the front of the quilt. You can use the usual 50wt thread for stitching or make it bolder using a thicker thread. Here I used the 35wt that I had sewn the quilt with. When you get to the corners, ensure you stitch the mitre in place with one stitch going over the fold (refer to image 4a, right).

4 When you complete the quilt, finish as for method 1, opposite. You will have a neat topstitched line of sewing on the front of the quilt (4a), and on the back a line of stitching running close to the binding seam (4b).

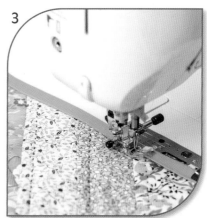

Hand-stitched variation of method 2

This method can be completed by hand using big stitch quilting as shown here and as used for the cathedral windows mini quilt on page 93. I used a 12wt thread for this – the same as for the quilting.

This method of QAYG works well for hand-quilted blocks. There is a margin or frame around each of the blocks and this is left unquilted before the blocks are joined together. Once joined, the area can be quilted according to the quilting design. The joining of the blocks is a three-step process, making a flat seam, which is easy to quilt over and almost invisible on the back. This is a very versatile method, as the design possibilities with the combination of blocks, fabric selection and frames is almost endless. It is also a very portable method; the joining can all be done by hand (but often people choose to do the first stage on the machine), the hand quilting finished on each row, and then the next row made and joined. For this reason it is often termed 'quilting on the go'.

The block chosen for this quilt – the sunbeam block – has some of its elements incorporated into the frame, blurring the distinction between the two. The block is based on an old design from the 1930s called 'Sun Beam'. A similar block is seen in 1939 in 'The Kansas City Star' – it is called the 'Thrifty Wife' block. It uses small amounts of precious prints, thus being thrifty with your fabric. Here, I have given you the fabric needed to make one block. Should you wish to make an entire 16-block quilt, refer to page 34 for instructions and complete fabric requirements.

MEASUREMENTS

Block size: 12in (30.5cm) square without frame, 16in (40.5cm) finished with frame

REQUIREMENTS FOR ONE BLOCK

Print fabric: One Fat Quarter (22 x 20in/56 x 51cm)

White fabric: One strip, 4in (10cm) by WoF

Frames: One strip, 5in (13cm) by WoF

Wadding/batting: 19 x 19in (48.25 x 48.25cm)

Backing: 19 x 19in (48.25 x 48.25cm)

Notions: Templates A, B, C, D, E and F (see pages 142 and 143)

Freezer paper for appliqué

Blending thread for the appliqué

No.12 perle cotton for big stitch quilting

No.6 embroidery or betweens needle

FABRIC CUTTING

Print fabric: C x 4, A x 4, D x 4

White fabric: B x 4, BR x 4, 10 x 10cm (4 x 4in) square for F

Frames: Cut 4 x ER and 4 x E

Creating a block

These blocks can be sewn by hand or machine, but the basic order remains the same. If machine-piecing, press all the seam allowances (SA) open. If working by hand, press in a consistent direction after piecing the block.

1 Use template F to cut out a freezer-paper circle. Iron this, shiny side down, to the WS of the fabric F square. Cut out, adding a scant ¼in (5mm) SA. Turn the SA over and tack/baste in place.

2 Pair up A and BR, wrong sides (WS) together and stitch. Make four. Pair up C and B, WS together and stitch. Make four.

3 Pair two units (an A-BR and a C-B) WS together and stitch. Make four.

4 Stitch the four units together to create a square with a hole at the centre. Press.

5 To make the frames, stitch E and ER to either side of D. Press the seams open. Make four.

6 Pin a frame to one side of the block, matching up D and C. Start stitching ¼in (5mm) from the edge of the block and stop ¼in (5mm) from the other end.

7 Repeat for the other three sides. Now stitch the mitre at each corner. Start by pinning two of the edges together.

8 Stitch the two edges together. Start ¼in (5mm) from the edge, which is where your previous line of stitching ended.

9 Press the seam open. Repeat to mitre all four corners.

10 To appliqué the centre, fold F into quarters and crease it; also crease the background square. Line up the creases to ensure that F is centred. Pin perpendicular to the edges of F, then slipstitch in place. Remove the tacking/basting and freezer paper.

11 Layer with wadding/batting and backing and tack/baste, ready to quilt. Whichever way you tack/baste (I used tacking/basting pins), remember to tack/baste ¼in (5mm) in from the edge, all the way around the outside edge. This keeps the block nice and straight, ready for joining. I used perle cotton no.12 to big stitch quilt. Outline quilt ¼in (5mm) from the seams, and within the centre circle. In the frames, quilt ¼in (5mm) from the SA, but stop quilting when you reach D. Leave the thread there as you can pick it up later when you join the blocks.

12 If you want to bind your block, select your method from pages 20–25. To make a larger quilt, learn to join blocks together on page 30, and then follow the instructions for the quilt project on page 34.

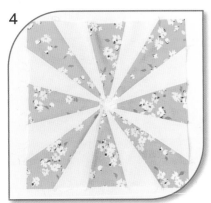

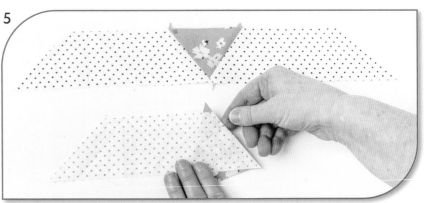

6

7

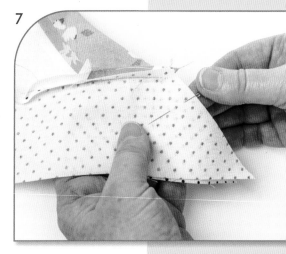

8

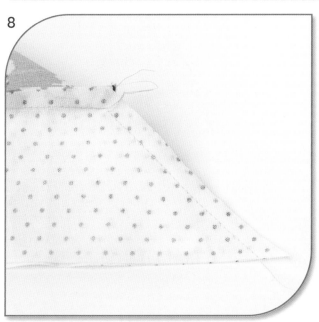

9

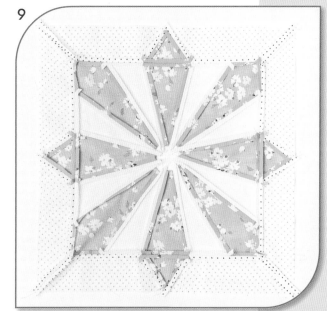

10

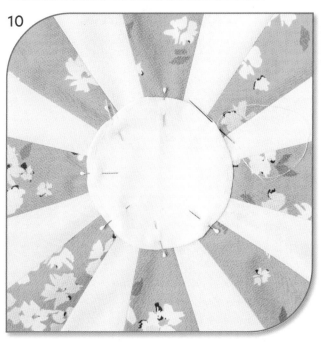

11

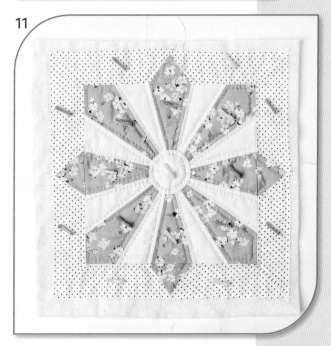

STITCHING BLOCKS IN A ROW

If you plan to make more than one block, the following pages will show you how to join them together. By using the quilting-on-the-go method, each row can be constructed and then the gaps between the row's blocks are quilted. When each row is complete, the rows can then be stitched together in the same way. The instructions for making up a row are here; to join the completed rows see page 32. This method can only be used if the block quilting stops 2in (5cm) from the edges, as for the block on pages 28–29. If you have quilted your blocks right up to the edges you can join them using one of the methods on pages 40 or 48.

1 Remove the tacking/basting from the sides of the blocks that you will be joining in order to separate the three layers of each.

2 Stitch the two blocks (the front of the quilt) together RS facing using a ¼in (5mm) SA. Within each row, press the seams in the same direction (alternate the direction in subsequent rows). So as not to unnecessarily press the wadding/batting at the same time, put the seam along the edge of the ironing board.

3 To trim away the excess wadding/batting, flatten the wadding/batting down first in the direction of the pressed seam, then lay the second piece on top. Using scissors, run the edge of the blade along the ditch of the seam and cut through both layers of wadding/batting at the same time. This will help to ensure that the edges will fit together and the join will be directly above the seam on the front of the quilt. Remove the trimmed wadding/batting strips.

4 To join the wadding/batting edges you can either use iron-on batting tape or stitch by hand (if using the tape, follow the manufacturer's instructions). To stitch by hand, use a neutral thread colour that will not show through the front of your quilt. Choose a stitch that evenly pulls both sides of the wadding/batting together and allows them to lay flat. Start with a knot and a backstitch to secure the thread in the wadding/batting and then bring the needle up on one side of the wadding/batting from the centre. Repeat this motion of coming up from the centre and alternating left and right. In this way, the stitch evenly pulls the edges together. Finish off with a few backstitches in the wadding/batting to secure.

5 Next you need to trim the backing fabric. Fold each side back along the seamline, RS together, so that the butted edges meet along the wadding/batting seam. Trim each edge of fabric to leave a generous ¼in (5mm) SA.

6 You will be making a seam with these two fabric edges, the bulk of which will lie in the opposite direction to the seam on the front of the quilt. This ensures a flat finish and it is easy to quilt over this area. First, flatten down the fabric that lies on the same side as the bulk of the seam on the front. Then turn a hem with the second piece, so the fold sits in the ditch of the seam on the front of the quilt. You can feel this with your finger. Pin from the centre of the seam out towards each raw edge.

7 Now use a slipstitch or similar to stitch down the seam. Be careful not to catch the first and last 2in (5cm), as this will need to be moved when you join further rows. If you do catch the wadding/batting, it can be easily snipped away from the stitching later.

8 Complete the row of blocks in the same way and then fill in any quilting between the blocks. If the row is on an outside edge of the quilt, you can continue any quilting up to the outside edges of the quilt at this stage. Complete any subsequent rows in the same way. For information on how to join your rows together, see pages 32–33.

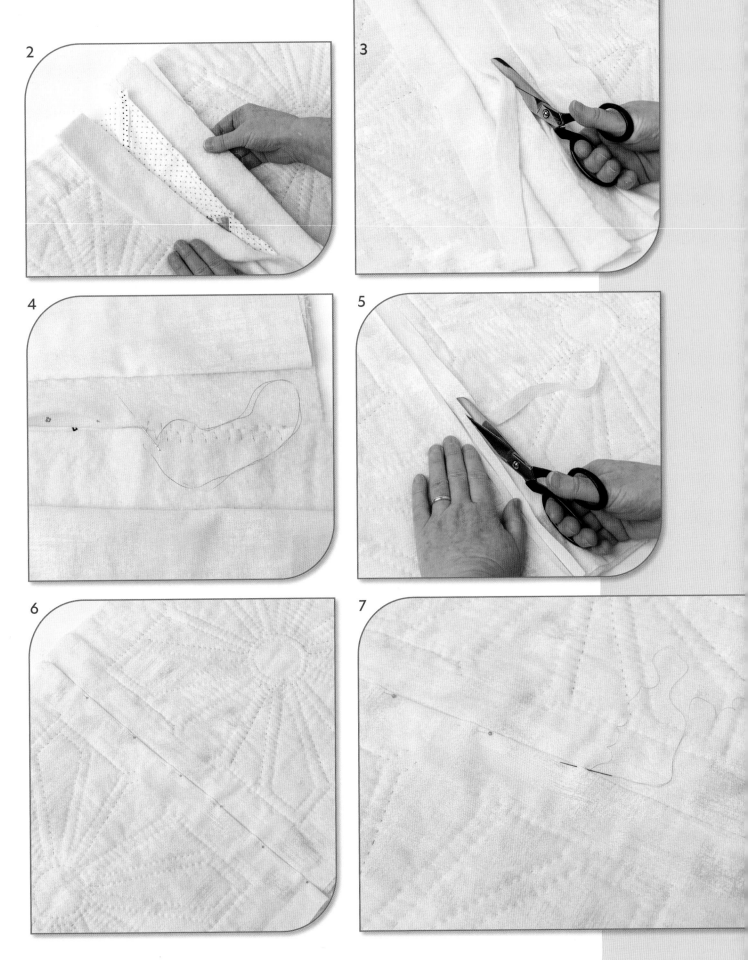

STITCHING ROWS TOGETHER

1 This is really just a longer version of the seams you have been sewing to attach the blocks to each other on pages 30–31.

2 Start by pinning the front seams of the blocks together at the start, end and at each junction where the seams will meet. Pin in between if you need to and then machine sew along the length of the seam.

3 Press the seam in one direction. It can be the same direction for all of the subsequent rows.

4 Trim and join the wadding/batting as in steps 3 and 4 on page 30 so that the edges butt together. If you have stitched the wadding/batting previously and now end up cutting through some stitching, don't worry, as you can re-stitch as you join the long seam, or iron it together with wadding/batting tape.

5 When it comes to trimming and joining the backing fabric, trim as in step 5 on page 30 to leave a ¼in (5mm) SA on each side.

6 Flatten one side of the seam and fold the other so that the bulk of the SA will be nested into the SA on the front of the quilt. This way, as before, there is no extra bulk to quilt through.

7 When pinning the seam on the back, I usually start at the junction points so that these will line up without distorting. Once you have pinned from these points and everything is flat you can start stitching from one end and work through to the other.

8 Once the row is complete you can fill in the quilting. In this way, as you stitch and quilt the rows, the quilt becomes complete!

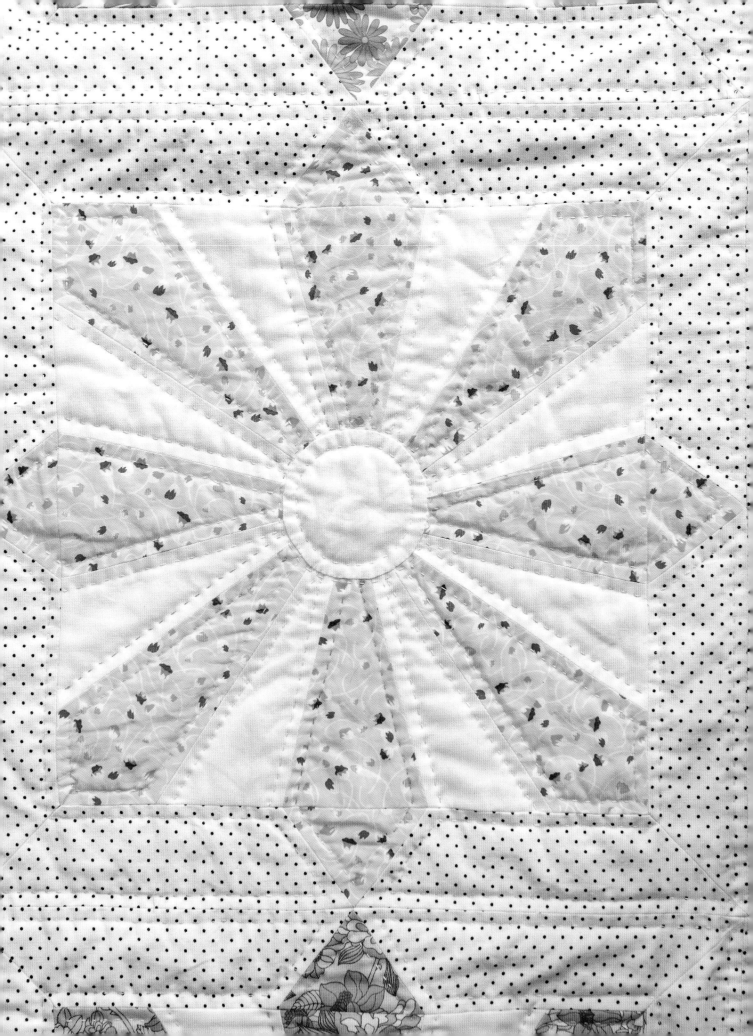

TURNING THE BLOCKS INTO A QUILT

For this full-size quilt you will need to make up 16 blocks using the fabric requirements, right, and the instructions on pages 28–29. Next, create four rows of four blocks using the method on pages 30–31. Once the rows are created, fill in the quilting; I quilted ¼in (5mm) each side of the seams. Then you will need to stitch the four rows together, following the instructions on pages 32–33, again continuing the quilting. When the quilt is constructed it can be bound (see pages 20–25). To finish, I then quilted around the outside edge of the quilt ¼in (5mm) from the binding.

MEASUREMENTS

Quilt size: 64 x 64in (163 x 163cm)

Block size: 12in (30.5cm) square without frame, 16in (40.5cm) finished with frame

REQUIREMENTS

Print fabric: Sixteen Fat Quarters (22 x 20in/56 x 51cm)

White fabric: 36in (91.5cm) by WoF

Frames: 80in (2.1m) by WoF

Wadding/batting: Sixteen 19in (48.25cm) squares

Binding: 18in (46cm) by WoF

Backing: 152in (3.9m) by WoF; a small all-over non-directional print works well if you want to hide the seams

Notions: Templates A, B, C, D, E, F (see pages 142 and 143)

Freezer paper and a blending thread for the appliqué

No.12 perle cotton for big stitch quilting

No.6 embroidery or betweens needle

FABRIC CUTTING

Print fabric per block (x 16): C x 4, A x 4, D x 4

White fabric per block (x 16): F x 1, B x 4, BR x 4

Frames per block (x 16): Cut 4 x ER and 4 x E per block (in total 64 of each). If you cut the fabric into 2½in (6.5cm) wide strips x WoF, this should yield 2 x E and 2 x ER

Backing: Cut sixteen 19in (48.25cm) squares

Binding: Cut seven strips, 2½in (6.5cm) x WoF. Join with bias joins to a continuous length, and press WS together along the length

2 Stitch-and-flip

This block uses the stitch-and-flip method or quilt-as-you-sew method of stitching. The block is pieced and stitched to the wadding/batting and backing fabric at the same time. You could add rows of machine quilting to the blocks or use big stitch hand quilting. Stitching lines of multicoloured herringbone stitch give this block an extra textural dimension. To make this as a full quilt, see pages 44–45.

The way that this block is constructed means that the stitching goes right up to the edge and so you can't use the method given for the previous quilt to join your blocks. Instead, the blocks are joined with strips of fabric, either just on the back (see page 40) or on the front and the back (see page 48).

MEASUREMENTS

Block size: 12 x 12in (30.5 x 30.5cm)

REQUIREMENTS PER BLOCK

Fabric strips: See fabric cutting, below

Fabric scraps: Two scraps, approximately 6 x 3½in (15.25 x 9cm)

Wadding/batting: 13 x 13in (33 x 33cm) square; I usually use a pure cotton, bamboo or soya wadding/batting as the cotton fabrics seem to stick to it without the need for any tacking/basting or pinning

Backing fabric: 13 x 13in (33 x 33cm) square

Notions: Walking foot or even-feed foot for the sewing machine

12½in (32cm) square ruler

Stranded embroidery thread/floss for the herringbone stitch or perle cotton no.12 for big stitch quilting, and a no.5 embroidery or quilting needle

Rotary cutter for wadding/batting so as not to dull the blade of the one you use for fabric, or remember to change your blade when trimming the blocks

Sewing thread for the machine to blend with the backing fabric if you do not want it to show

FABRIC CUTTING

Fabric strips: I don't usually pre-cut these, but if you are more organized than me, a block uses roughly: one 19 x 2½in (48.25 x 6.5cm) strip; two 16 x 2½in (40.5 x 6.5cm) strips; two 13 x 2½in (33 x 6.5cm) strips; two 10 x 2½in (25.5 x 6.5cm) strips

Fabric scraps: I don't like to have lots of seams on the corners of these blocks, so I fill the last corner section in with a bigger piece. Your pieces might be bigger or smaller than mine depending on your blocks and the SA

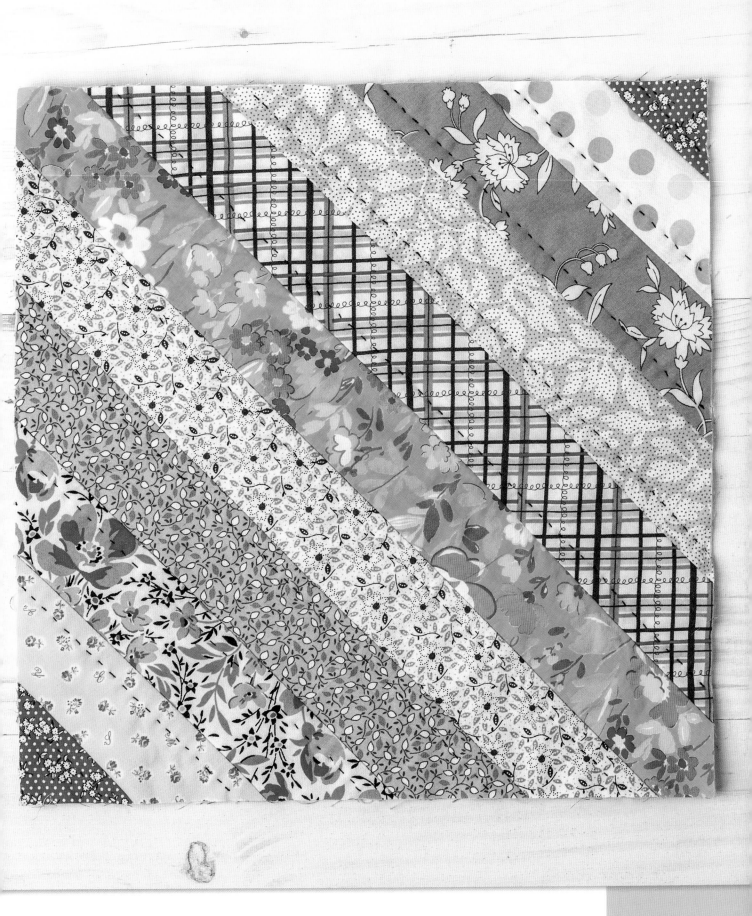

Creating a block

1 Place the backing fabric square wrong side (WS) up and the wadding/batting square on top. I don't tack/baste this as I find they tend to stick to each other anyway. Now place a long strip diagonally from corner to corner, right side (RS) up on the wadding/batting. I do this by eye and don't measure. The centre of the strip should be roughly in the centre of each corner of the square.

2 Place a second strip RS down on top of the centre strip, raw edges together. Machine stitch along the lower edge of the strip with the usual ¼in (5mm) SA. You are stitching through the two strips, the wadding/batting and the backing fabric. All of the strip placement is done by eye. None of the strips are meant to match perfectly when the blocks go together.

3 Flip the strip open.

4 Repeat the same process on the other edge of the first strip. Open out the two strips and press.

5 Repeat this process with the rest of the strips until you are near the corners of the block (I found it took four strips each side of the centre strip to reach this point). You don't want to have too small a piece in the last corners of the block as this will create a lot of bulk at the joining stage; use the larger scraps to fill in the last corners, and press.

6 Now trim the block to 12½in (31.75cm) square. The wadding/batting and the backing will have distorted a little during the sewing process, so you will be trimming these off as well as the front strips.

7 At this point you can add big stitch quilting (as shown on page 37), or herringbone stitch (as shown here and on page 41). To keep the scrappy feel I used dozens of different colours, but you could choose just one, or a variegated thread. I have just stitched over the SA of each strip, using three strands of embroidery thread/floss in my needle. Remember to hide the knot and the thread ends in the wadding/batting as you stitch, just as you would if you were hand quilting (see page 19).

8 You can now go ahead and bind the block (see pages 20-25). Alternatively, you can make a complete quilt, such as the one outlined on pages 44-45, making 25 blocks and joining them first into rows. Two methods are given for this. Method 1 (pages 40-43) uses fabric strips on the quilt back to cover the seams; method 2 (pages 48-51) uses strips on both sides, turning them into a decorative feature.

1

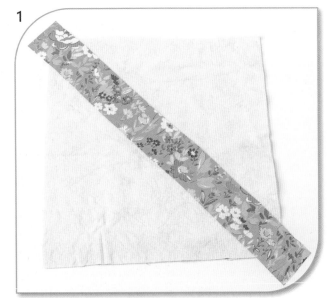

2

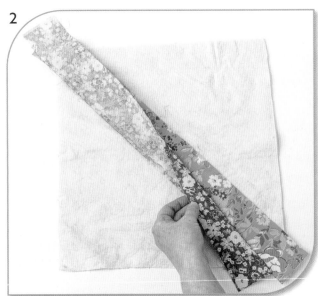

JOINING THE BLOCKS: **METHOD 1**

This method of joining stitch-and-flip blocks together is great for any QAYG blocks that are quilted all the way up to the raw edges. The resulting finish looks just like a normal seam on the front of the quilt (see above, opposite), and has a strip of fabric covering the seams on the back of the quilt (see below, opposite). The fabric strips can be the same fabric to blend in or contrast for a quirky finish. Equally, they could all be cut from completely different fabrics for a very scrappy look which would be great for using up odd ends of fabric.

The blocks are machine-sewn together and the strip of fabric is hand-finished on the back of the quilt. This means that the seam is slightly bulkier than usual, but is strong and, as with all quilts, it will soften up with use. If you don't wish to do any hand finishing, see method 2 on page 48, which can be done completely on the machine.

REQUIREMENTS

Stitch-and-flip blocks: Your desired number. Prepare the blocks so that they are all pieced and quilted to the wadding/batting and backing fabric. Trim off the excess and square them all up to the necessary size according to your quilt project.

Fabric strips: The joining strips to cover the seams on the back are cut to 2¼in (5.75cm) wide, and generally a few inches longer than the seam they will cover. This extra will be trimmed off later. Press the fabric strips in half along the length, WS together. If strips need joining, use a bias join, as this distributes the bulk better and makes for a neater and stronger finish.

Notions: Hand-sewing thread to blend with the strips on the back of the quilt

Hand-sewing needles, sharps no.10

Fabric clips to hold the seams together

The joined fabric blocks from the front (above, opposite) and the back (below, opposite).

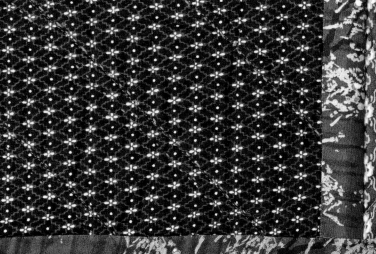

Joining the blocks

1 To stitch the blocks together, place a pair of trimmed blocks RS together and place a short joining strip on top, with the raw edges aligning. Your strip should already be folded in half lengthways. Leave a small amount of the strip overhanging at the start and finish of the seam. Use fabric clips to hold these together.

2 Machine along the seam as normal, stitching the blocks and the strip together.

3 Open out the blocks and flatten the seam with your fingers away from the strip. Now fold the strip over the SA, flattening it all as you work so that the folded edge of the strip covers the raw edges. Smooth the seam flat and pin the strip in place.

4 Using a blending sewing thread, slipstitch the folded edge of the strip in place. Remove the pins. Repeat to join any remaining blocks in the row.

5 For the second row, start stitching the blocks together from the opposite end of the row. This way the SA will face the opposite way. Finish off the binding on all of the seams.

6 Now place the rows together, RS facing, pinning at the seam junctions – when you come to sew the rows together the SA will knit together nicely at the junctions (as shown).

7 Place the long seam strips on top of the facing rows (as you did for the blocks in step 1) before stitching the seam. Trim off any strip ends on the outside edge of the quilt.

8 Open out the rows and flatten down the strips to cover the raw edges. Stitch the binding down by hand as before. If you used a contrasting fabric for the binding strips, this will give a staggered grid effect on the back of the quilt.

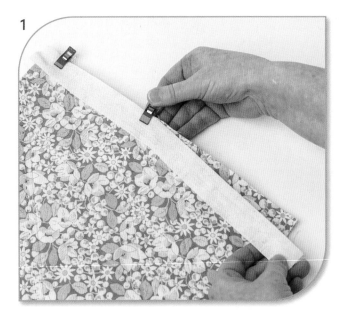

TURNING THE BLOCKS INTO A QUILT

Refer to the information below for the requirements for this quilt and to cut your fabrics. This quilt uses method 1 on pages 40–43 for joining the stitch-and-flip blocks together.

1 Make 25 blocks, following the instructions on pages 36–39.

2 Once the blocks are complete, place them in an arrangement that you are happy with. The diagonal strips lend themselves to a few designs, so have a play before committing. Place them in five rows of five blocks.

3 Using method 1 on pages 40–43, sew the quilt together in five rows of five blocks.

4 Once complete, bind the quilt to finish, choosing your binding method from pages 20-25.

REQUIREMENTS

Fabric strips: Sixty strips, 2½in (6.5cm) by WoF

Fabric scraps: Fifty scraps, approximately 6 x 3½in (15 x 9cm)

Wadding/batting: Twenty-five squares, 13 x 13in (33 x 33cm)

Backing fabric: 117in (3m) by WoF; you can use one fabric or lots of different ones. Lots of different fabrics along with contrast binding on the seams on the back of the quilt will create an almost double-sided type quilt

Seaming strips for backing: 30in (76cm) by WoF; this can be the same fabric as the backing if you do not want the seaming to show. If you use a contrast fabric, a grid effect of the seams is very visible

Binding: 18in (50cm) by WoF

Notions: walking or even-feed foot

12½in (32cm) square ruler

Stranded embroidery thread or perle cotton no.12 for big stitch quilting

No.5 embroidery or quilting needle

Rotary cutter

Sewing thread for the machine

FABRIC CUTTING

Fabric strips: Each block uses roughly: one 19 x 2½in (48.25 x 6.5cm) strip; two 16 x 2½in (40.5 x 6.5cm) strips; two 13 x 2½in (33 x 6.5cm) strips and two 10 x 2½in (25.5 x 6.5cm) strips

Fabric scraps: I don't like to have lots of seams on the corners of these blocks, so fill the last corner section in with a bigger piece. Your pieces might be bigger or smaller than mine depending on your blocks and the SA

Backing fabric: Twenty-five 13 x 13in (33 x 33cm) squares

Seaming strips for backing: Cut thirteen strips 2¼in (5.75cm) wide, trim the selvedge/selvage and join to a continuous length with bias joins to minimize bulk. Press the seams open. Cut twenty 2¼ x 13in (5.75 x 33cm) strips and four 2¼ x 62in (5.75 x 157.5cm), and press along the length, WS together

Binding: Seven WoF strips, 2½in (6.5cm) wide; join to a continuous length with bias joins and press WS together along the length

MEASUREMENTS

Quilt size: 60½ x 60½in (154 x 154cm)

Block size: 12 x 12in (30.5 x 30.5cm)

JOINING THE BLOCKS: **METHOD 2**

Like method 1 (see page 40), this technique can be used to join any QAYG blocks that are quilted all the way up to the raw edges – such as the Appliqué quilt shown on page 113. The resulting finish will have narrow (½in/1cm) strips of fabric on the front of the quilt and slightly wider (approximately ¾in/2cm) strips and visible machine stitching on the back. The fabric strips on the front of the quilt will form part of the quilt design, and the fabric selection should be made accordingly. They can be made to stand out or merge in with a background fabric – you can make this grid as bold or as minimal as you like. The fabric strips on the back can be the same fabric to blend in or contrast for a different look. Equally, they could all be cut from completely different fabrics for a very scrappy look.

The blocks are machine sewn together with strips of fabric on the front and back holding the blocks together with a flat seam. The block edges are butted together between the strips. It is worth noting that when you reach step 5, you can stitch the backing strip down by hand if you prefer. Use slipstitch to do this. The appliqué quilt on pages 112–113 uses this technique.

REQUIREMENTS

Stitch-and-flip blocks: Your desired number. Prepare the blocks so that they are all pieced and quilted to the wadding/batting and backing fabric. Trim off the excess and square them all up to the necessary size according to your quilt project

Fabric strips: The joining strips on the front are cut to 1in (2.5cm) wide, and generally a few inches longer than the seam they will cover. This extra will be trimmed off later. The strips for the back are cut 1½in (4cm) wide. If strips need joining, use a bias join, as this distributes the bulk better and makes for a neater and stronger finish. Use the usual ¼in (5mm) SA for all seams. Make sure there is enough fabric strip to protrude either end of each join. This ensures the fabric is long enough, so you won't get caught short. It will be trimmed off later.

Notions: Long, strong, sharp pins

Small fabric clips

Sewing thread to blend with the quilt for stitching in the ditch

The joined fabric blocks from the front (above, opposite) and the back (below, opposite).

Joining the blocks

1 Take the first block in the row to be joined and place the front strip RS together with the front of the block. Align the raw edges. Now put the backing strip along the same edge on the back, RS of the fabrics facing. The block will be sandwiched between the two strips. Hold together with fabric clips. Stitch along this seam, taking a ¼in (5mm) seam allowance.

2 Now take the second block and pin the front strip edge to the block, RS together.

3 Stitch along this seam. When done, open out the blocks to lie flat. The SA will be butted together between the two blocks.

4 Fold the backing strip WS together, so that the raw edge meets the machine-stitched seam line. Now fold this edge over to cover the butted seam – it will overlap the stitched seam line on the next block. Pin from the back using the long pins. Pin perpendicular to the seam. You may be able to see the pins from the front of the quilt, and this will help when it comes to removing them as you stitch.

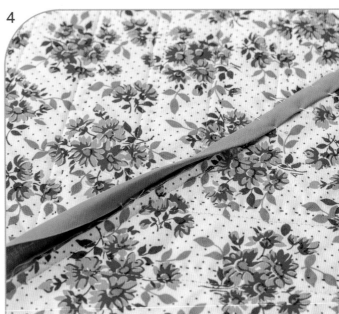

5 Now, stitching from the front of the quilt, sew in the ditch of the seam.

6 You will be sewing down the folded edge on the back of the quilt. As you sew, remove the pins from the back. Stitch slowly to ensure accuracy; removing the pins as you sew helps slow you down. On the front the stitches will be barely visible. On the back you will have a line of stitching close to the folded edge of the strip.

7 Rows of joined blocks are joined in exactly the same way. Make sure you match up the joining strips on the front of the quilt – the excess tabs of fabric will help you do this. Sew along the seam, then trim away the excess fabric ends.

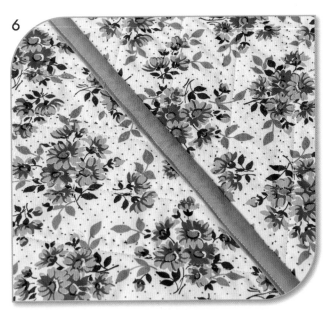

3 Piecemaker's quilting

This is a truly scrappy quilt, which can utilize very small pieces of fabric, even the off-cuts from quilts-in-progress: the fabric, backing and the wadding/batting pieces that you trim off before binding can really come into their own here. Save them up and those pieces can be sewn into a new quilt. This is a great quilt for a bit of machine stitching during the day, and then in the evening doing a bit of hand quilting on it in front of the TV. The next day you are ready for the next machined row.

The method focuses on stitching the front, back and wadding/batting together in rows or strips. As each row is completed, you can then add machine or hand quilting to that row, or leave it as it is. Then, when you have off-cuts for a second row, off you go.

For this technique, all the layers need to be cut into strips: not just the front but also the wadding/batting and the backing. If you work on this quilt as your scraps arise, it may take a while before the quilt is the size you want. I focused on my fabric strips being cut at 2½in (6.5cm) wide, but you could go slightly wider if you like to build up the quilt at a faster rate. But if you want to quicken the pace, use pre-cuts like Jelly Roll pieces at full length or cut up, use smaller 5in (13cm) Charm Squares cut in half, or cut a 10in (25.5cm) Layer Cake into four 2½in (6.5cm) strips.

Equally, the back of the quilt could be cut from one fabric or many different ones. I tend not to use fabrics for the back that need too many joins, as if these collide too often with the joins on the front it can result in some bulky lumps. Even when it comes to binding, you could use up left-over pieces from other quilts.

You could also make blocks with this method, like the square shown opposite, and join them together with one of the machine-joining techniques (see page 48).

REQUIREMENTS

Fabrics: See left

Notions: Sewing machine with a zigzag or overlock-style stitch (optional)

Seam roller

Fabric clips

Flat-headed pins: these don't create a bump, which can sometimes get in the way of the machine foot

Optional: Machine quilting thread

12wt cotton perle thread for hand quilting

JOINING THE STRIPS

1 To prepare for the making of the quilt, there are a few basics. Wadding/batting can be purchased in rolls already cut 2¼in (5.75cm) wide, and you can cut this to the length of the strips as you work. Or you can use up any oddments you have saved from other projects. I make the wadding/batting fractionally narrower than the fabric to slightly reduce the bulk in the SA. Cut your wadding/batting strips 2¼in (5.75cm) wide and trim the ends straight. You can now join these together. Use a neutral sewing thread in the machine and set the stitch to a medium zigzag. Butt the ends of the wadding/batting together, and machine them (see page 15). You might want to chain piece these, and snip them apart when finished. Fusible fabric tape (see page 15) is also available, but I feel that for such short pieces it is actually more trouble that sewing!

2 The fabrics you use are also useful if they are in long pieces. Cut the strips to 2½in (6.5cm) wide and join together the short ends with the usual ¼in (5mm) SA, pressing the seams open. If you like, you can use a bias join, and this will give the quilt some interesting angles (see page 20). Decide on the length of the strips. For the quilt on pages 56–57 I used strips 60in (152.5cm) long, but select your length depending on the size of quilt you want.

3 To start, lay a backing strip WS up. Place a wadding/batting strip on top, centrally. Place a front strip on top, RS up. Use pins to hold the three layers together. This strip sandwich is the start of the quilt and your first row.

4 Now place it on top of a backing strip, with the backing strips RS together. Hold in place with some fabric clips.

5 With the front of the quilt strip facing you, lay a front strip RS down, and a wadding/batting strip on top. Secure with fabric clips.

6 Stitch along the sandwich raw edge with the usual ¼in (5mm) SA, or the width of your presser foot. If you use the normal presser foot, the seam may be a little wider, but that doesn't really matter here. Remove the clips as you work.

7 Now stitch along the raw edge with a medium zigzag stitch. This keeps the SA from being puffy and adds some extra stability (see opposite). If you prefer, use an overlock-style stitch, so that you only need to stitch the seam once.

8 You can now fold the two added fabrics WS together with the wadding/batting in the middle. Use a seam roller in lieu of pressing and make sure that the two raw edges of the back and front fabric strips match up. Use the flat-headed pins from the first row to keep this new (second) row together.

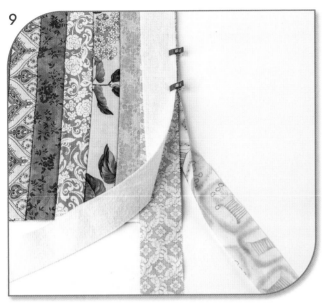

9

9 You are now ready to add the next row in the same way. Place a backing strip RS up, then place the raw edge of the quilt on top. Place a fabric strip RS down, then add a wadding/batting strip on top. If you like, you can switch ends to start from for each row, as this can stop the rows becoming uneven or bowing. Sew this next row in place, zigzagging or overlocking/serging the seams, if you want to. Then fold the strips out and press.

10 Continue on for as many rows as you like. Remember that after each row is complete you have the option to add machine quilting, use a decorative stitch or do some hand quilting. I do this once each row has been encased by the next. This way, by the time the machine sewing is complete, the quilt is also quilted too.

11 Once finished, trim to straighten up the sides and then bind using your chosen method (see pages 20–25).

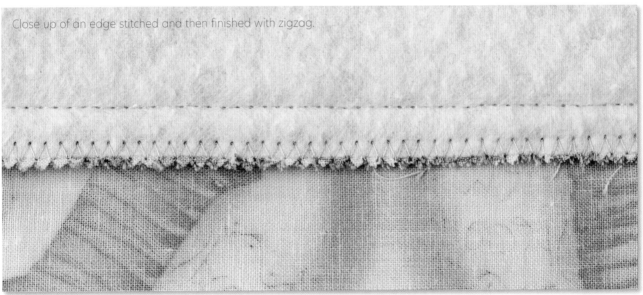

Close up of an edge stitched and then finished with zigzag.

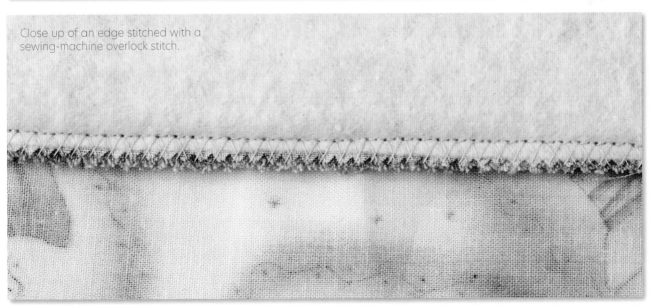

Close up of an edge stitched with a sewing-machine overlock stitch.

TURNING THE STRIPS INTO A QUILT

1 To stitch, follow the basic method on pages 54–55. I organized my backing strips before starting to stitch. This way they were ready to go without having to spend time referring to what I had already stitched. You can keep them flat by hanging them from a coat hanger.

2 Once I had stitched all of my front fabric strips together into one long length, I wrapped it around the length of a fabric bolt inner board. This kept the strip flat and I could wind off a length when I needed it.

3 I hand-quilted using big stitch Mennonite tacks and cotton perle thread after each few rows were encased.

4 I stitched 23 rows for this quilt. When the quilt was finished, I straightened it up along the sides, and then bound it using continuous mitred binding (see page 21).

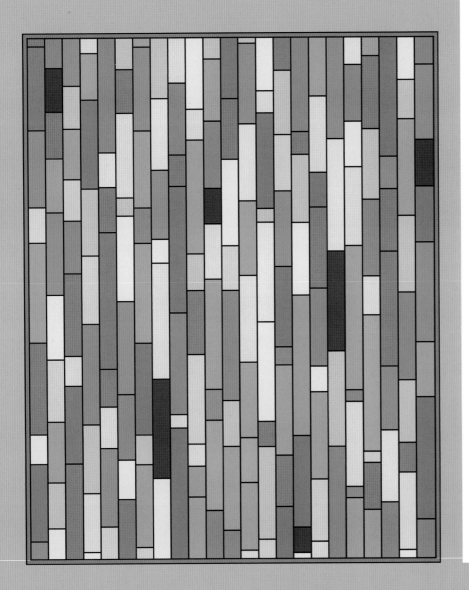

MEASUREMENTS

Quilt size: 57 x 46in
(145 x 117cm)

REQUIREMENTS

Fabric scraps: One Jelly Roll would be enough to make this quilt

OR dive into your scrap bag and use thirty-six strips of fabric, cut 2½in (6.5cm) x WoF

Backing: I used one fabric, 90in (2.25m) by WoF. If you want to cut the backing strips parallel to the selvedge/ selvage, you will need 120in (305cm) by WoF; cut into two lengths of 60in (152.5cm) then cut twenty-three strips. There will be leftovers with this method

OR use a selection of fabrics: three 60in (152.5cm) strips of fabric joined to a continuous length and then cut in half will give two backing strips

Wadding/batting: Pre-cut batting 2¼in (5.75cm) wide

OR off-cuts of spare wadding/ batting to join

OR 52 x 60in (132 x 152.5cm)

Binding: 15in (40cm) by WoF. Join to a continuous length with bias joins, fold along the length WS together then press

Notions: Seam roller

12wt perle cotton for hand quilting

Flat-headed pins

Fabric clips

▶▶ 4 Manx log cabin

TRADITIONAL:
BY HAND OR MACHINE

Traditionally this style of patchwork is entirely hand-pieced, and no measurements are given, as each piece is dependent on the size of the makers' own hands. These are used as a gauge, and all the fabric is then snipped and ripped. The technique originates in the Isle of Man, hence its name. There is no wadding/batting required, and the texture is created by the folds in the 'logs' as you sew. These folds help create insulation and warmth. In a way, this is the ultimate QAYG technique, as it can be measured, made and stitched absolutely anywhere. For the 15 x 15in (38 x 38cm) mini quilt on pages 62–63 you will make and join four blocks. For a larger quilt, see page 64.

Measuring up

In order to make your blocks you will need to know the measurements of your hand listed below. Make a note if you wish to then stitch the blocks by machine or cut the fabrics with a rotary cutter.

Base fabric/backing = hand span.

Centre square = length of middle finger.

Log width = length of thumb (tip to knuckle joint).

REQUIREMENTS

Fabric for logs: Cotton fabric, craft cotton, dress-weight cotton, and/or washed and pressed fabric from old clothes you may want to recycle. The design works well if there is a contrast between the light and the dark logs of the block, but this is not always necessary depending on what you have or how you want to interpret the design. Any colour scheme is great. I suggest Fat Quarters, or long quarter metres, and any scraps you may wish to incorporate. Each block has a circuit of four logs, and you can use one light and one dark fabric throughout or four light and four dark fabrics.

Block centres: Traditionally red, but use whatever you are happy with

Backing: This is the back of your blocks and you will be sewing through it by hand. Cotton flannel or brushed cotton is nice, as it is slightly sturdier and soft. Craft cotton and dress-weight fabric is good, but I think Tana lawn, although good for the logs, is too fine for the backing

Binding: 5in (13cm) by WoF. Cut two 2½in (6.5cm) strips by WoF. Join to a continuous length with a bias join. Press WS together along the length

Notions: Fabric-cutting scissors

Basic sewing kit, including small scissors, pins, thimbles etc.

Sharps no.10 or no.11

Neutral colour sewing thread to blend with the backing fabric (I prefer 28wt for hand sewing)

Seam roller (useful if you don't want to use the iron)

A small rotary cutting mat, or sheet of sandpaper can be useful if using a seam roller to stabilize the fabrics

Making a 4-patch mini quilt

1 Snip and tear a strip of backing fabric. The measurement is your hand span. Snip and tear into a square. Repeat to make the centre square using the measurement of your middle finger. Fold and finger press the base square diagonally both ways. Line up your centre square, with the corners sitting on the diagonal lines, to centre it. Pin in place.

2 On each side of the base square, fold the raw edge in to meet the raw edge of the centre square. Finger press or seam roller this line. You can iron this in place if you have an iron. Now fold the raw edge to meet the creased line, and crease the new line. Now fold the middle line to meet the centre square raw edge and crease the line. You now have a grid to guide your sewing.

3 Snip and tear or cut 'log' fabrics as you need them. Starting with the light fabric, cut a piece the length of the centre square. Match up the raw edges and place it wrong sides together on the central square. Stitch a seam ¼in (5mm) from the raw edge. If you are sewing by hand, you can just approximate where the seam should sit; start with a knot (this will be on the side of the work that faces you, not left exposed on the back), and a backstitch. When you reach the end of the seam, leave the threaded needle on the back of the work. It is less traditional but also perfectly valid to sew these seams on the machine, should you prefer!

4 Fold the stitched log WS together so the raw edge is in line with the first creased line. Pin in place.

5 Cut and align the next light-coloured log and (if hand sewing) bring the needle up ready to stitch the ¼in (5mm) seam. It will not be at the start of the log, and that is fine.

6 Continue to stitch and fold logs around each side of the square. For the second two logs, use your darker fabric. At the end of the first round of logs you can finish off and cut the thread, leaving the thread tail on the inside of the log.

7 Continue on in the same order until the last round of logs. Make sure you do not stitch to the raw edge of the base fabric here, but always leave at least ¼in (5mm) of the log free (7a). This will help when you join the blocks together. When each block is finished, put a pin in each outer log to keep the fold in place until you are ready to join the blocks together (7b). Make the other three quilt blocks in the same way.

8 Work out your chosen mini quilt arrangement. To join two blocks together, put the blocks RS together. Pin the fronts only together (as shown). Stitch a ¼in (5mm) seam from raw edge to raw edge.

9 Press in one direction. The seam roller works well on this narrow seam.

10 Flatten the backing fabric in the opposite direction to the pressed seam. Fold over the remaining SA so that it covers the flattened SA. You can usually feel how the fold on the back knits in with the seam pressing on the front. Pin in place and stitch down with a slipstitch or hemming stitch. Stitch from raw edge to raw edge, catching the backing fabric only.

11 Repeat with the second pair, this time pressing the SA in the opposite direction.

12 Now you can stitch the two pairs together. You will find that the seams will knit together neatly at the junction. Again, stitch the front together first, then press and stitch the backing. Once together, the mini quilt can be bound (see pages 20–25).

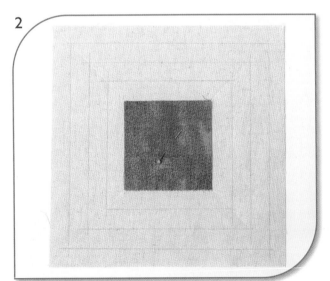

2

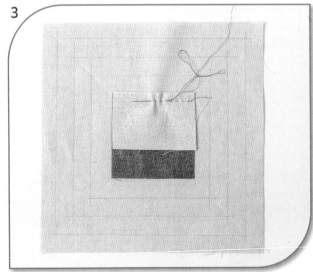

3

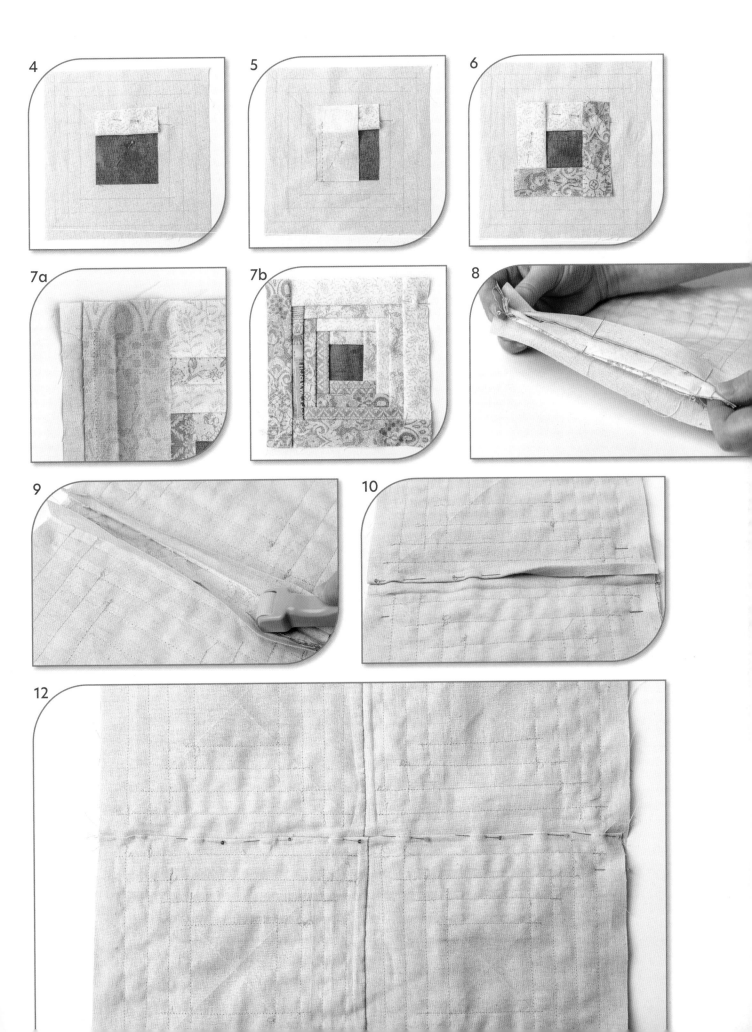

TURNING THE BLOCKS INTO A QUILT

This time-saving variation of the traditional log cabin design is sewn on the sewing machine. I also cut all of the fabrics using my rotary cutter.

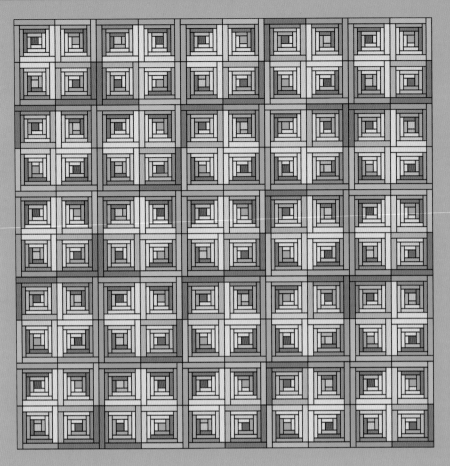

Measuring up

Length of middle finger (centre square) = 3in (7.5cm)
Top of thumb to knuckle joint (strip width) = 2in (5cm)
Hand span, stretched (backing/base fabric square) = 8in (20.5cm)

MEASUREMENTS

Quilt size: 75in (191cm) square

Block size: 7½in (19cm) square

REQUIREMENTS

Fabric logs in assorted colours: For a scrappy look, allow 2in (5cm) by WoF per block. This quilt has 100 blocks, so 200in (5.2m) in total. If you want to allow a bit extra, 224in (5.7m) will give you flexibility

Fabric logs in cream: For a scrappy look, allow 2in (5cm) x WoF per block. This quilt has 100 blocks, so 200in (5.2m) in total. If you want to allow a bit extra, 224in (5.7m) will give you more flexibility

Backing fabric: 160in (4.1m) by WoF

Centre squares: If you use one fabric, 24in (65cm); if you want to go scrappy, 3in (7.5cm) by WoF yields thirteen 3in (7.5cm) squares

Binding: 20in (55cm) by WoF

Notions: 1 x 12in (2.5 x 30.5cm) rotary cutting ruler

Pencil to mark fabric OR Hera marker

Fabric scissors

¼in (5mm) piecing machine foot

Sewing thread to blend with the back of the quilt

FABRIC CUTTING

Fabric logs in assorted colours: Cut 100–112 lengths, 2in (5cm) by WoF

Fabric logs in cream: Cut 100–112 lengths, 2in (5cm) by WoF

Backing fabric: Cut twenty strips, 8in (20.5cm) by WoF. Sub-cut to create 100 8in (20.5cm) squares

Centre squares: Cut eight strips, 3in (7.5cm) by WoF. Sub-cut to create 100 3in (7.5cm) squares

Binding: Cut eight strips, 2½in (6.5cm) by WoF. Join to a continuous length with bias joins and press in half WS together along the length

64

Making the quilt

1 Make up your Manx log cabin blocks using the measurements on pages 64–65 and the instructions on pages 62–63, this time stitching on the machine. I cut the strips to length as I sewed, and used securing stitches at the start and finish of each seam. Clip all the threads on the backing fabric close to the fabric. You can also stitch to the end of each log on the first three circuits.

2 For the first log on the fourth (last) circuit, stitch end to end. For the remaining three logs, remember not to stitch all of the way to the edge of the base fabric, but to leave a ¼in (5mm) margin to allow for the blocks to be joined later.

3 I joined the single blocks together into twenty-five four-patch blocks, following the instructions on pages 62–63. (Alternatively, you can join them row by row: 10 rows by 10 blocks.)

4 You will now need to stitch five of the four-patch blocks into a row. Again, try to alternate the seam direction, but if some don't work out due to fabric placement on the front, the quilt will still go together even if some seams do collide. Repeat for the other four rows of five. You can stitch the fronts together on the sewing machine, but the joining of the backs is still best done by hand. (If joining the blocks in rows, remember to alternate the direction of the seams, so that they knit together.)

5 Join the five rows together in the same way.

6 Once all of the rows are together, the quilt can be bound. To help reinforce the edges I stitched a narrow zigzag all the way around the outside of the quilt before binding. I bound the quilt using standard continuous mitred binding, which I hand finished (see page 21).

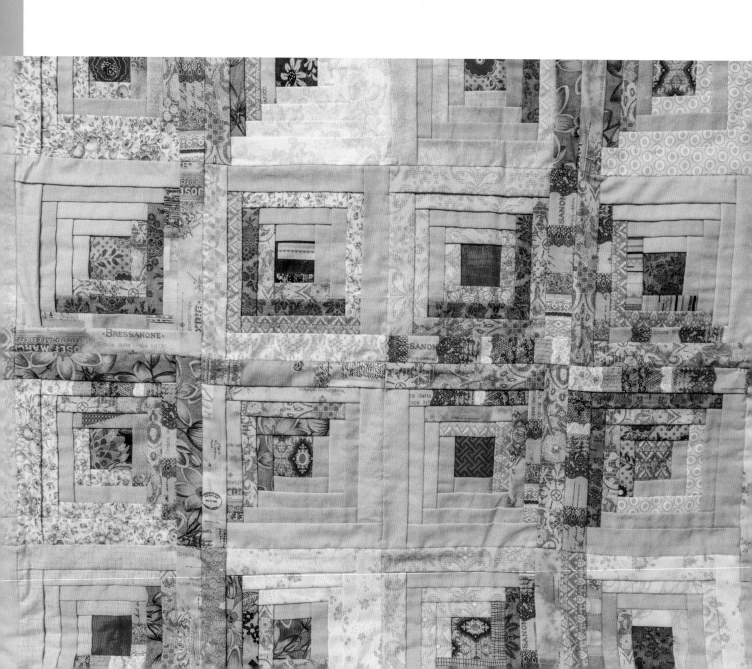

MODERN MANX LOG CABIN

To bring the process up-to-date, and to make use of the speed the tools and materials today can offer, I have adapted the design to stitch on the sewing machine, using a pre-printed grid to guide the sewing lines. The strips are quickly cut with rotary cutting tools and pieced on a sewing machine. This block size works well as a tablemat, a mini quilt or even a doll's quilt. If you want to use it as tablemat or coaster, I suggest you add a layer of heat-resistant wadding/batting between the backing fabric and the pre-printed grid before starting to stitch. You can use any of the classic layouts for the Manx log cabin block (see page 69 for some further inspiration).

MEASUREMENTS

Block size: 9½in (24cm) square

REQUIREMENTS

Backing fabric: 10in (25.5cm) square

Centre square: 2in (5cm) square

Fabric for logs in cream: 6in (15cm) by WoF

Fabric for logs in assorted colours: Assorted plain colours – ten or more if you do not want repeats. A pre-cut Layer Cake works well, as you get a nice choice and the squares are the right size for the backing

Wadding/batting (optional): Vlieseline heat-resistant wadding/batting, V272 Thermolam or cotton wadding/batting square; 10in (25.5cm) square

Binding: 6in (15cm) by WoF

Notions: Machine sewing thread, 50wt, in a colour to blend with the backing fabric

Vlieseline Quickscreen: Rasterquick 453, 10 x 10in (25 x 25cm)

Rotary cutter, mat and ruler

Fine patchwork pins

A 9½in (24cm) square ruler is useful, but not essential, for squaring up

Temporary fabric adhesive spray (optional)

Glue stick (optional)

FABRIC CUTTING

Fabric logs in cream: Three strips, 1½in (4cm) wide

Fabric logs in assorted colours: 1½in (4cm) wide strips with a maximum length of 10in (25.5cm)

Binding: Two strips, 2½ x 12in (6.5 x 30.5cm)

Two strips, 2½ x 10in (6.5 x 25.5cm)

Making the block

1 Centre the pre-printed background grid on the WS of the backing fabric. If you are adding wadding/batting, sandwich this between the two squares. Pin the layers together at each corner to stop them shifting, or use a spray baste to hold them together.

2 Place the 2in (5cm) centre square RS up in the centre of the grid, you can count the units to work this out and pin in place, or use a glue stick. If you want an off-centre log cabin, place the square towards one corner of the block: it's up to you, there are so many options!

3 Cut two 2in (5cm) long strips of cream to start stitching with. This is the only time that I pre-measure the strips – for the rest of the stitching I trim as I stitch, following the lines on the grid.

4 Place a cream strip RS together, raw edges aligned, on the centre square. Use a ¼in (5mm) SA to stitch through all the layers. Note that if you don't use a ¼in (5mm) SA and just use your regular sewing machine foot, all that happens is that your pleat will be slightly shallower, so don't worry too much! Start and stop your stitches by reversing to secure them, then snip the threads on the backing fabric. There are no threads to tie off: the seams will be secure, as the next rows of stitching cross the last ones, adding extra security.

5 Repeat on the opposite side of the centre square with the second strip of cream.

6 Now unfold each cream strip and line up the raw edge with the next visible vertical line on the grid. I use a pin placed perpendicular to the raw edge to secure it until the next line of sewing does that job.

7 With two coloured strips (for my first colour I chose purple), repeat steps 4–6, to attach, pin back and thus complete the first round.

8 Repeat this process to complete the second round; I kept my cream logs vertical, and used yellow for my second colour.

9 Repeat this process for eight further rounds, until the grid is covered; I trim the fabric as I sew from here on. As you work you can see the pleats being created. What I like about this way of working the technique is that if your fabric is flat and pressed from the cutting, then there is no more pressing to do as you sew!

10 When the square is filled, neaten the edges and square up to 9½ x 9½in (24 x 24cm). I then stitch all the way around the outside edge of the block ⅛in (3mm) in from the raw edge to keep all of the layers together. Bind using square-cornered binding (see page 23).

2
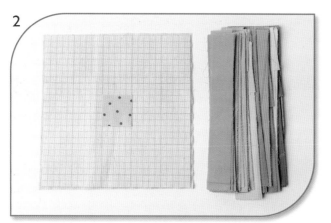

5
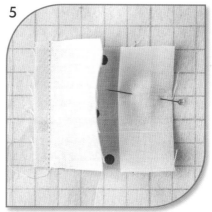

6
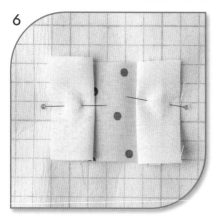

7
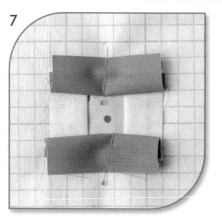

8
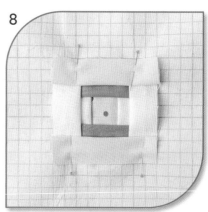

Below: three possible
fabric arrangements.

▶▶ 5 Potholder quilting

This type of quilt has existed since 1856 or even earlier. A potholder quilt is characterized by patchwork blocks that are stitched, quilted, often signed and then bound before being sewn together to make one whole quilt. The quilts were sometimes friendship or presentation quilts, but a large number documented were made during the US Civil War (12th April 1861–9th April 1865). These were made by women to help raise funds or to donate to hospitals for injured soldiers. They are a great example of a QAYG and friendship quilt all in one. The name is thought to have come from the custom of quilting and binding squares of fabric and wadding/batting to make an insulated pad to hold the handle of a pot, kettle or casserole, hence 'potholder'.

Insights into a group project:

Group quilts and friendship quilts are always a lovely idea, and it seemed appropriate to talk about that at some stage in a book about QAYG. The key to this sort of project is the organization. Generally, folks want to do the right thing (i.e. sew the block the right size in the right colours, by the date you need it!) so the more information you give, the better the end result will be.

- I felt that the wadding/batting and backing fabric needed to be consistent for this quilt, but I didn't want people having to buy stuff they might not already have. So each participant was sent: wadding/batting, backing fabric, embroidery thread, quilting thread and needles.
- The sizing of the blocks is an important factor, in order for them all to fit together, so this is a good one-person job.
- Binding them was also done by one person for consistency, but the hand finishing could have been done by many individuals. Equally, time allowing, sewing them together could have been delegated too. Think about these things when you plan the quilt and you will be off to a good start.
- Think about the block you want to use and how this will look with the thin band of binding between the blocks. Also consider the skill level and how the block will be made. I selected a block that could be stitched by hand or machine, and did not contain any set-in seams. It is also quite a bold block, and could have had the makers' names in each block. However, I asked for names to be embroidered on the backing, to give people more room, and so that they did not need to worry about their stitching being scrutinized on the front.

Dear Quilt Group,

I'm writing a book, and in it I'd like to include an example of this method of Quilt as you Go from the 1860s and Civil War period in the US. If you search for potholder quilts online you will get an idea of the type of quilt: blocks stitched and quilted, individually bound and then stitched together. I'd like for it to be a group quilt, so I am asking some of my stitching friends if they would like to contribute a block...

I am supplying the pattern instructions, backing fabric, wadding/batting square and the quilting thread (with two needles). There will be cutting instructions in the pack and guidelines for the piecing and quilting, which I would like in the big stitch style, hence the cotton perle supplied. The block size is 12½in (31.75cm) finished (13in/33cm raw edge to raw edge). You can hand or machine piece.

You will need to make the block from a low-volume fabric and a navy/blue fabric. There can be other colours in the prints, but I would like the overall scheme to be blue.

I would like you to write/sign your name on the BACKING fabric before you layer and quilt the block, and embroider it. Nothing fancy – running stitch, backstitch or chain stitch will all be great. All the signed names will be on the back of the quilt. There is stranded cotton included in the pack, and I usually use three strands.

Along with the finished quilted block, you will also need to supply me with two strips of the blue fabric used in your block, cut 2½in (6.5cm) wide by the width of the fabric. I will use this to bind a block, but not your block!

Carolyn xx

Right: an example of the letter I sent out to everyone I asked to participate.

When the blocks were collected, it was lovely to see the cards and messages that people had added...

... and extra fabrics for binding, just in case they were needed.

POTHOLDER QUILT BLOCK:
GREEK CROSS VARIATION

1 Following the diagrams, stitch the block together, pressing as indicated.

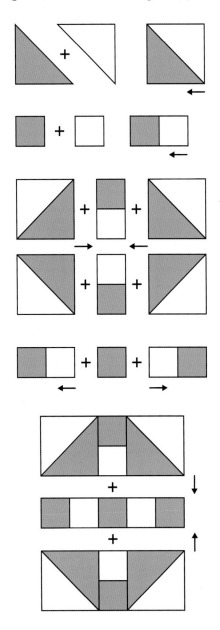

2 Embroider your name in the middle on the RS of the backing fabric using two or three strands of the embroidery thread, and whichever stitch you like.

3 Layer the block, wadding/batting and backing fabric, then tack/baste together ready to quilt.

4 Mark the quilting lines. I use a Hera marker, but pencils or chalk all work well. The grid of cross-hatching is based on the construction of the block so is straightforward. The quilting is in the ditch along the diagonals of the HSTs (so no need to mark!) and the next is 1¾in (4.5cm) away. Quilt using the cotton perle and big stitch quilting.

MEASUREMENTS

Block size: 12½in (31.75cm) square; 13in (33cm) square raw edge to raw edge

REQUIREMENTS

Blue fabric: 13in (33cm) x WoF. Use blue prints, not a plain fabric. They can have other colours in, but the overall look should be blue. You can use scraps, and there can be more than one print in the block if you don't have enough

Low-volume fabric: 6in (15cm) x WoF. This can be a plain or print, just so long as it contrasts with the blue you choose

FABRIC CUTTING

Blue: Two strips, 2½in (6.5cm) by WoF (for binding)

Two squares, $5\,^7/_8$ x $5\,^7/_8$in (15 x 15cm); sub-cut into four half-square triangles (HST)

Four squares, 3 x 3in (7.5 x 7.5cm)

Low-volume: Two squares, $5\,^7/_8$ x $5\,^7/_8$in (15 x 15cm); sub-cut into four half-square triangles (HST)

Five squares, 3 x 3in (7.5 x 7.5cm)

Each participant was sent:

A 15in (38cm) square of backing fabric

A 15in (38cm) square of wadding/batting

Perle cotton no.12 for quilting

No.6 quilting and embroidery needle

Stranded embroidery cotton in a shade of green

TURNING THE BLOCKS INTO A QUILT

1 This quilt is made using 25 of the potholder quilt blocks (see pages 72-73) in a five-by-five grid.

2 Trim the selvedges/selvages off the binding strips. Join the binding strips together with a bias join, pressing the seam open. Now press the entire length of the strip, WS together and set aside.

3 Once your blocks are quilted, start to square them up. Although in theory they should all be squared up to 13in (33cm), you will no doubt find you have variations. I always go with the smallest size, and square them all up to that.

4 Plan your layout, photograph and label the blocks. I then allocate the bindings that have come in with the blocks to different blocks. Just pop the binding fabric on top of the blocks as they lay, and you will get a good idea as to how things will look. This will help get a good mix of the different fabrics throughout the quilt.

5 Now bind all of the blocks. I used the mitred binding on page 21.

6 They can now be stitched into rows. I used whipstitch and 40wt sewing thread. Whipstitch seemed to be most common on the old quilts so I went with that, keeping with tradition. You could also use a zigzag stitch on the machine. It is often easier to hold the blocks together with fabric clips than pins, as they keep the blocks flat when held together.

7 Once the rows are together, the quilt is complete, and already bound and labelled!

MEASUREMENTS

Quilt size: 62.5in (159cm) square

Block size: 12½in (31.75cm) square

REQUIREMENTS

Blue Fabric for blocks: 132in (335cm) x WoF

Low-volume fabric for blocks: 126in (320cm) x WoF

Backing fabric: 195in (495cm) by WoF

Wadding/batting: Twenty-five 15in (38cm) squares

Binding: 80in (203cm) by WoF

Notions: Perle cotton no.12 for quilting

No.6 quilting and embroidery needle

Stranded embroidery cotton in a shade of green

FABRIC CUTTING

Blue fabric: Cut ten strips, 3in (7.5cm) by WoF. Sub-cut 125 3in (7.5cm) squares

Cut seventeen strips, 5⅞in (15cm) by WoF. Sub-cut fifty 5⅞in (15cm) squares. Sub-cut 100 HST

Low-volume: Cut eight strips, 3in (7.5cm) by WoF. Sub-cut 100 3in (7.5cm) squares

Cut seventeen strips, 5⅞in (15cm) by WoF. Sub-cut fifty 5⅞in (15cm) squares. Sub-cut 100 HST

Backing fabric: Cut thirteen strips, 15in (38cm) by WoF. Sub-cut into 15in (38cm) squares

Binding: Cut thirty-two strips, 2½in (6.5cm) by WoF. Join with bias joins to make a continuous length; press along the length WS together

Contributors to the potholder quilt:

Tracy Aplin
Stephanie Bunt
Madeline Cline
Tracey Dawkins
Janette Dodd
Marion Drake
Nicky Eglinton
Carolyn Forster
Elle Gager
Veronica Greenslade
Lizzie Gripper
Jenny Groves-Gidney
Jenny Holmes
Sandra James
Belinda Jeffries
Natalie Jones
Florence Knapp
Mary O'Riordan
Tansy Martin
Loulou Peaches
Jane Ricketts
Schehrezade Sanderson
Catriona Saville-Smith
Jane Spedding
plus maker unknown

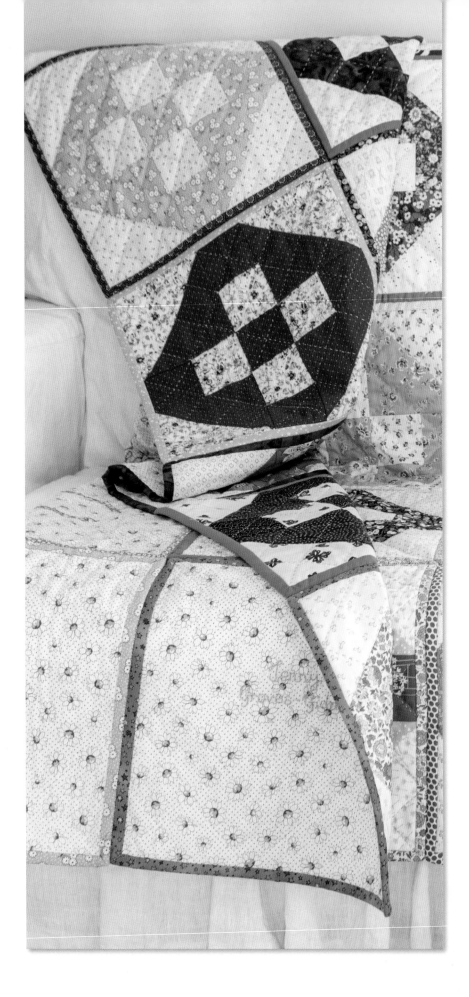

6 Japanese reversible patchwork

The technique of finishing off the raw edge of a quilted patchwork piece is not new – many old quilts have the backing turned over to the front in order to finish off the quilt. What is different about this Japanese method is that the patches have their edges finished before they are sewn into a quilt. Plus, the patches were developed to include circles and other shapes so as to create new and interesting designs.

Some Japanese books on the process became popular in the 1980s, for example, those written by Sachiyo Muraki. These books showed in great detail through diagrams and pictures just how many possibilites for stitchery this process offers. Not only were quilts made this way, but many bags, mats and sewing trinkets. Many Japanese women found the neatness of the process, the amount of design possibilities and the small scale, manageability and portability of the work all very appealing.

Traditionally, this Japanese patchwork was stitched by hand utilizing fine hand quilting, but this can be adapted to use big stitch quilting and also some machine work. Popular shapes include circles wrapped around squares, diamonds and triangles, hexagons wrapped around hexagons in two ways, and circles or squares wrapped around squares.

Hand-stitched methods:

I have used the classic hand-stitched method for the quilt project on pages 82-83. I have used a 12wt thread for the quilting of the patch and the same weight for the classic joining stitch. This method can be adapted to use fine hand quilting (28wt thread) and using a whipstitch or over-sewing stitch to join the patches. Equally, ladder stitch can be used to hold the patches together.

Machine method:

Although the quilt project on pages 82-83 is worked by hand, you can easily replace the hand stitching with machine stitching. When the bound edge is stitched in place you can use straight stitch or a decorative machine stitch to do this. These shapes are not too small, so not too fiddly to put under the machine. It is a great way to get to know your sewing machine and experiment with thread types.

When joining the shapes you can use a small zigzag stitch or even a hemming stitch, but make sure you secure the thread ends. Have a practice on some samples - you can always use them as coasters if they don't make it into the quilt.

MEASUREMENTS

Block size: 5½in (14cm) point to point

REQUIREMENTS PER HEXAGON

Backing: 9in (23cm) square

Front fabric: 6in (15cm) square

Wadding/batting: 6in (15cm) square

Notions: Fabric clips

12wt thread

Size 6 embroidery or betweens needles

Templates: large and small hexagons (see page 141)

FABRIC CUTTING

Backing: Cut the large hexagon using the template

Front fabric: Cut the small hexagon using the template

Wadding/batting: Cut the small hexagon using the template

Making the block

1 Layer a small hexagon (front fabric) RS up on top of a wadding/batting piece. Place this centrally on the WS of the large hexagon (backing fabric). You can line up the straight of grain on the two fabrics, but it will not matter too much if you don't.

2 Fold one edge of the backing fabric over to meet the raw edge of the front fabric and wadding/batting.

3 Fold again to cover the front fabric hexagon, like a binding. Pin in place with a fabric clip or a pin.

4 Working clockwise around the hexagon, fold the second side in the same way. You will automatically create a neat mitre at the corner.

5 Continue all the way round until you are on the last side. You will see that all of the corner folds go in the same direction until the last one. You can leave this (5a), or re-fold that corner to match the others (5b).

Alternative folding method

An alternative folding method is to fold over every other side: three to start with (A). Then fold the remaining three (B).This gives you symmetrically folded corners without having to do a refold. You can use either method.

6 Once the edging is bound, hold in place with a running stitch through all of the layers. This in effect is big stitch quilting using the 12wt thread. Stitch close to the folded edge so that it does not flap up, and make sure you catch down the fold at each corner. You can work a stitch along the corner folds.

7 I have not quilted inside the hexagon once bound, but there is nothing to stop you, depending on your fabric and design choices. I tend to work on lots of these and wait until I have a pile before I start to put them together into something larger.

5a

5b

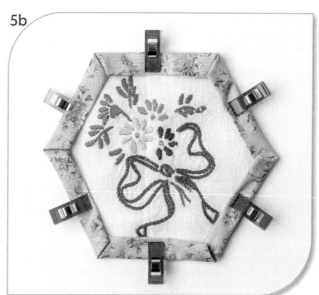

Alternative folding method

A

B

6

TURNING THE BLOCKS INTO A QUILT

Hexagons are a classic in the world of patchwork, and the binding on these adds a fun dimension. You can approach this as you would any hexagon quilt with plans and sketches as to the layout; you can make any design that you would with the usual hexagon shape, including the somewhat scrappy version that I have done here.

I repurposed old embroidered tray cloths and table linen for the front of my quilt, and raided my scrap bag for the back. Some of the old cloths had no embroidery in some areas but I have still cut hexagons from that and used it in parts of my design. If you have not got linens to cut up, use fabric prints with a largely white background – often termed low-volume prints – to give a similar effect. Alternatively, you may want to use one fabric for the back and lots of different prints for the front. The scope is endless.

For this quilt, I started in the centre and have worked in circuits. There are five circuits, and I used plain white fabrics for circuit 2. I used a 12wt thread to stitch the hexagons together (I used a baseball stitch, but you could use another stitch if you prefer). Hide the knotted thread in the wadding/batting as you would for quilting, and finish in the same way. Once your design is complete, there is no need to bind, as the patches already have a finished edge.

For information on making this quilt by machine, see page 78.

MEASUREMENTS

Quilt size: 56in (142.5cm), point to point

Block size: 5½in (14cm), point to point

REQUIREMENTS

Backing: Twenty-three Fat Quarters OR nineteen fabric strips, 8½in (21.5cm) by WoF

Front fabric: Eleven Fat Quarters OR thirteen fabric strips, 5in (12.75cm) by WoF

Wadding/batting: 56in x 56in (142.5 x 142.5cm)

Notions: Fabric clips

12wt thread

Size 6 embroidery or betweens needles

Templates: large and small hexagons (see page 141)

FABRIC CUTTING

Backing: Cut ninety-one large hexagons using the template

Front fabric: Cut ninety-one small hexagons using the template

Wadding/batting: Cut ninety-one small hexagons. Use a small hexagon cut from fabric as the template, as this often makes the cutting easier and there is no need to draw around it before cutting

Hint:

Look out for rotary cutting templates for the hexagon shapes. This can cut down on the time spent cutting the fabrics and wadding/batting, especially when used with a turntable-cutting mat

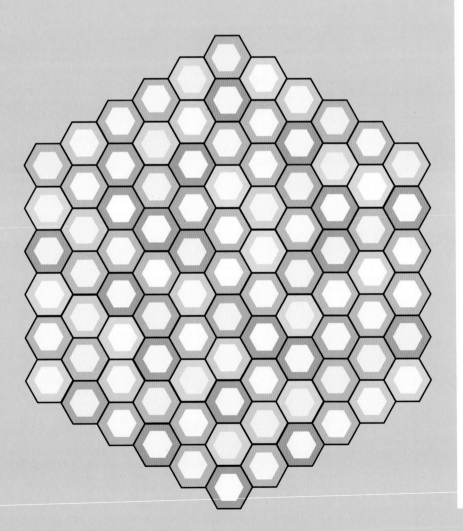

ALTERNATIVE BLOCK OPTIONS

A selection of blocks sampling the different ways the technique can be used. These include hexagons wrapped around hexagons to form a star, circles around triangles, squares and diamonds and pieced squares around squares. Some shapes will make borders around the shapes, and others will cover the wadding/batting totally without the need for a front fabric.

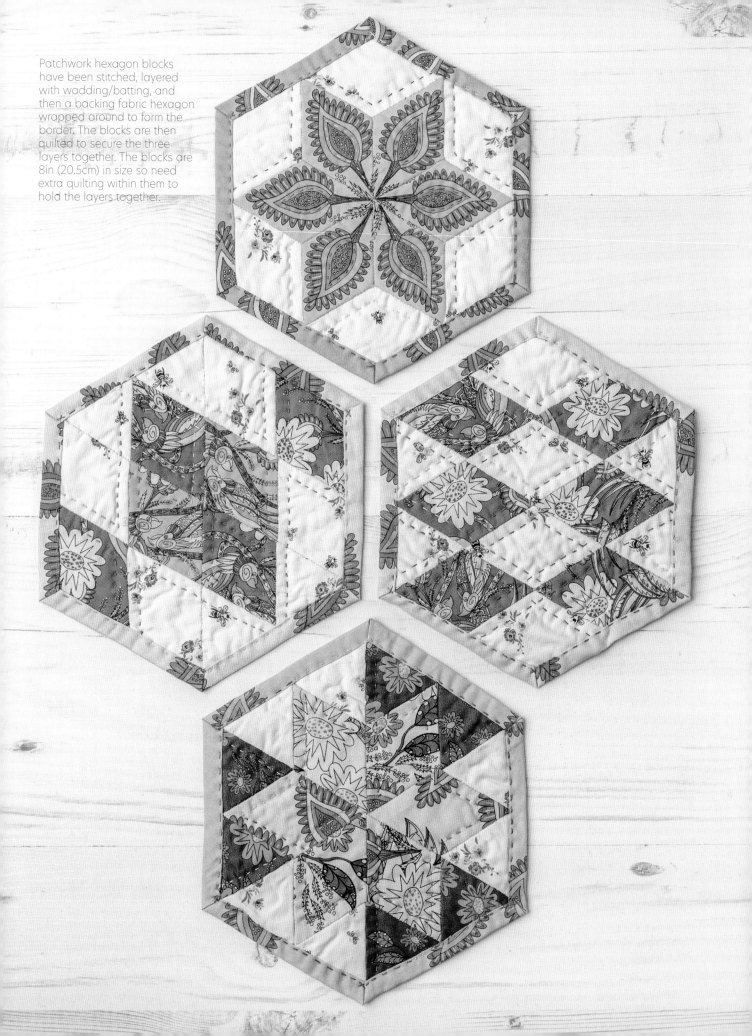

Patchwork hexagon blocks have been stitched, layered with wadding/batting, and then a backing fabric hexagon wrapped around to form the border. The blocks are then quilted to secure the three layers together. The blocks are 8in (20.5cm) in size so need extra quilting within them to hold the layers together.

▶▶ 7 Envelope quilting

This fun technique makes double-sided quarter-square triangles (QST) or Hourglass patches, which are quilted before they are stitched together into a quilt. Because each patch already has finished edges, there is no need to bind a quilt made from them, although you will find that binding adds extra stability.

Machine sew the patches then hand or machine quilt them. If I am making up patches into a larger quilt, I try to work on the machine sewing in a big batch, and then have the task of turning through the patches with the wadding/batting inside while I'm watching TV, as it's not the most exciting part of the quiltmaking. Once this is done, I can then do the hand-work at my leisure. QAYG techniques are meant to help make the process of quilt-making easier, and I find working in big batches suits me.

This idea was developed from samples of old quilts and an article written by Margaret Gutowsky in *Quiltmaker* magazine (July/August 1998). You can make the finished quilt (see pages 90–91) in as many or as few colours as you like.

MEASUREMENTS

Block size: 6¼ x 6¼in (16 x 16cm)

REQUIREMENTS FOR ONE POCKET

Fabric: Four 5in (13cm) squares

Wadding/batting: One 6¼in (16cm) square

Notions: Fabric glue stick

Template plastic

Sewing thread to blend

Point turner and seam creaser tool or similar (such as a wooden chopstick)

Quilting template (see page 141)

MAKING A QAYG ENVELOPE

1 Make a four-patch block as follows. Stitch two pairs of 5in (13cm) squares RS together. Press the SA in opposite directions, and then join the two pairs together, neatly knitting the seams together in the middle. Press the central (just stitched) seam open.

2 Fold each unit in half, RS together, along the pressed-open seam. Along one end (here, the right-hand side), stitch from top to bottom. At the other end (here, the left-hand side), stitch in the same way but leaving a gap in the middle of about 1½in (4cm). Secure the threads so they will not unravel.

3 Now pull the unit apart, as shown, matching up the raw edges and the centre seams.

4 Stitch the entire length of this open edge. Press the long seam open and you now have your square.

5 Place the square of wadding/batting on the side of the unit that has not got the gap in the seam. You might want to use some dabs of glue stick along the SA to help the wadding/batting stay in place.

6 Turn the unit RS out through the gap in the seam. Sometimes it helps to poke the corner furthest from the gap through first, then the rest will follow.

7 Make sure the wadding/batting is flat and poke the corners out square. Slipstitch the gap with blending thread.

8 Mark the quilting design using the template and quilt each patch to finish.

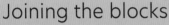

Joining the blocks

Once you have completed steps 1–8, the unit can be stitched together with others to form a quilt or other items, should you wish. There are four main ways to stitch the units.

- Depending on your sewing machine you may be able to butt the edges of the blocks together and use a suitable stitch to sew them together.

- Using a blending thread, hold the patches RS together and use a hand oversewing stitch or whipstitch (see opposite).

- Using a blending thread, hold the patches RS together and use a hand ladder stitch to hold the patches together invisibly.

- Using a stronger and bolder-coloured thread, use a decorative hand stitch to hold them together, such as baseball stitch.

Sew the units together in the chosen way, in rows or blocks, then sew the rows together. You can leave the quilt as it is or you might want to bind the outer edge. For more information on making a quilt from these blocks, see pages 90–91.

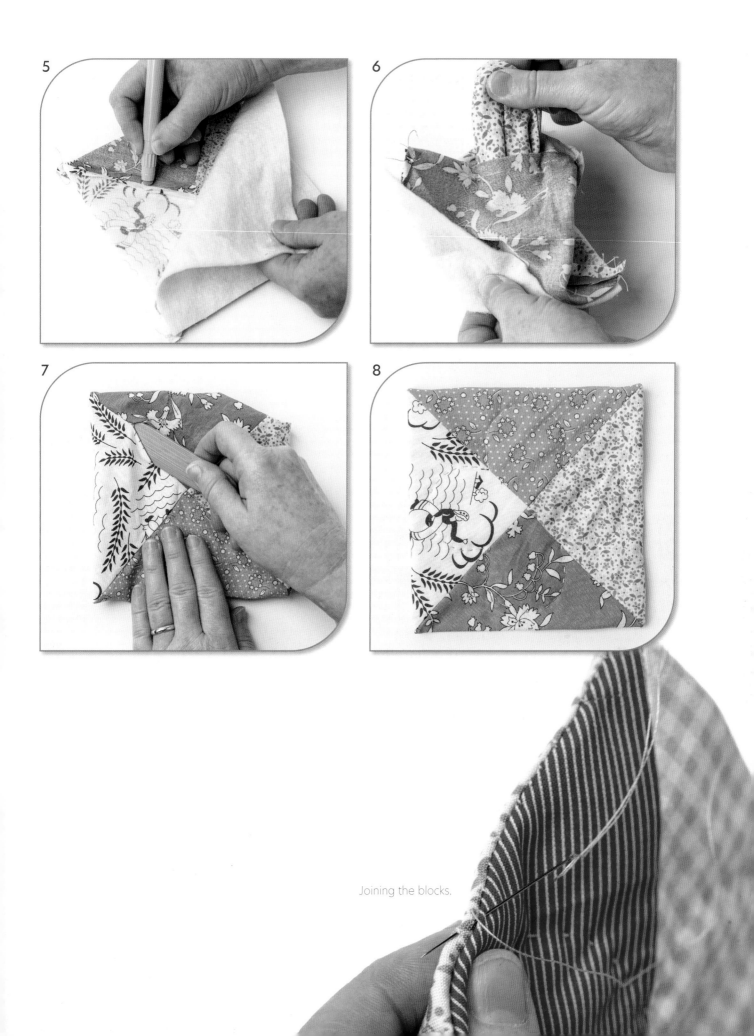

Joining the blocks.

This quilt is a real stash-buster, with a whole range of fabrics included. I made the quilt in blocks of four, and if you look closely you can see that the alternate blocks in the rows have a black print pinwheel. I machine-stitched and then big stitch-quilted them before sewing them together by hand with ladder stitch. All the seams are ¼in (5mm).

MEASUREMENTS

Block size: 6¼in (16cm) square

Quilt size: 62½in (160cm) square

REQUIREMENTS

Light/low-volume prints: For a scrappy look, cut 5in (13cm) by WoF from twenty-five different prints

OR use 200 Charm Squares

OR use one print, 125in (3.25m) by WoF

Black print for pinwheels: 35in (90cm) by WoF

Medium/dark prints: cut 5in (13cm) by WoF from nineteen different prints

OR use 148 Charm Squares

OR use one print, 95in (2.45m)

Wadding/batting: 100 6¼in (16cm) squares. Pure cotton wadding/batting or an 80/20 blend work best as they tend to 'stick' to the cotton fabrics

Binding: 18in (50cm) by WoF – this can be the same fabric as for the pinwheels as it adds a nice consistency. Cut seven 2½in (6.5cm) strips by WoF. Join to a continuous length with bias joins and fold and press along the length WS together

Notions: Fabric glue stick

Quilting template (see page 141)

Fabric clips

Optional: template plastic for quilting design

50wt machine sewing thread to blend

Thicker (40wt) thread for joining the blocks

Point turner tool or similar

FABRIC CUTTING

Light/low volume prints: Cut 200 5in (13cm) squares

Black print for pinwheels: Cut fifty-two 5in (13cm) squares (the yield is fifty-six so there will be four left over)

Medium/dark prints: Cut 148 5in (13cm) squares (the yield is 152 so there will be four left over)

1 To make the 48 scrappy envelopes (the ones without the black pinwheels), stitch the fabrics into envelopes, following the instructions on pages 88-89. Try to use two lighter fabrics and two darker fabrics in each one to highlight the pattern.

2 When you have made the 48 envelopes and quilted them, they are ready to stitch together into 12 four-patch blocks. Lay them out as in the diagram so they make a pinwheel design. It will be subtle in these blocks as there is less contrast

than for the black pinwheel fabrics. I used ladder stitch to join my patches and I find fabric clips useful to hold them together when sewing.

3 Now make 52 pockets as before, this time incorporating one of your black pinwheel squares into each one, before finishing and quilting them.

4 Lay them out in the same pinwheel pattern, so all of the black print fabrics go in the same direction as the darker fabrics in the previous blocks. Stitch together.

5 Lay out the first row of five four-pocket blocks, starting and ending with a black pinwheel block. Stitch together, using the fabric clips to secure them whilst stitching.

6 The second row starts with a scrappy block. Continue building up these alternating rows until all five rows are complete.

7 Next, stitch the rows together.

8 Although the edge is finished, if you want to make the quilt a little more durable, bind it to finish (see pages 20-25).

8 Cathedral windows

Cathedral windows blocks consist of a base fabric folded into units and joined. Then the bias edges of the units are folded over to cover the raw edges of the upper fabric, forming the windows. Despite the simplicity of the process, many designs and variations can be created, and the thickness of the fabric layers creates a textured and weighty quilt. There is no wadding/batting, but the layers of fabrics, and the stitches holding the window fabrics in place, make for a cosy and quilted patchwork.

The sizes of the base squares can vary, but I have worked mine in a large square, which means the process is not fiddly – you can use Charm Squares for the fabric windows and yet the quilt is still portable to stitch. This method creates a coverlet, as there is no wadding/batting, but it fits nicely into the QAYG family, as the stitching that holds the windows in place goes through all of the fabric layers and creates a quilted effect all in one go.

The quilt can be worked in rows, and as these rows get added to the main quilt, the windows are stitched in place, so you are always hand-stitching on the row closest to you. The stitching is all worked in one direction along each row (right to left if you are right-handed and left to right if you are left-handed).

Fabrics for the windows can be patchwork-weight cottons, but the base fabric should be something lighter in weight. Because of the number of layers you will need to stitch through, and to achieve a good finish, I use a fine lawn or, in the case of the quilt project on pages 96–97, a lightweight cotton gingham.

This style of patchwork was popular in the 1930s, and many examples can be seen with a white base cloth and colourful scrap patches in the windows. By using an inexpensive base cloth, more could be made of the prized scraps of fabrics for the windows. If you don't want to embark on a whole quilt, then make a mini quilt, which can be completed as fun table centre, mini quilt or made into a small pillow front (see pages 94–95).

MAKING A FOUR-BLOCK MINI QUILT

1 To make one base block you are essentially following the instructions for the envelopes on page 88, but using a single piece of fabric rather than a four-patch block. Take a backing square and fold it in half RS together. Stitch along each short end, but leaving a 2in (5cm) turning gap in the middle of one end. Now, holding the seams you just stitched, put them together and flatten the fabric to create a square with a long seam. Finger press the matching seams open and stitch completely along the long seam. Press all of the seams open.

2 Turn the square RS out, and press. The gap can be left, as it will be covered by fabric. Now press the four corners to the centre of the square. 2a shows the fold lines; 2b shows the corners folded to the centre. Make three further backing blocks in the same way.

3 To make a two-patch row, stitch two squares together, matching up the crease line, and with the flaps folded away from the centre. Secure the stitches at the start and finish. Make two rows of two squares.

4 Now stitch these rows together into a square. You will have a square with flappy triangles.

5 You now need to sew all of the flaps in place. You can do this by hand or by machine. On the machine, simply stitch ½in (1cm) from the point over to the opposite point then reverse. Snip the loose threads. Stitch the remaining two points in the same way. To hand-sew, stitch through all of the layers to hold the points in place (5a). The secured four-patch block is shown in 5b.

6 Now you can place the windows. Place the squares in the centre of each window. Place the triangles around the edge so that the raw edge is along the folded edge of the backing. On the small quilt here it does not matter about the order you stitch, but on a large quilt like the project on pages 96–97, it is helpful to work on one row at a time.

7 Turn over the edges of the triangle flaps so that they cover the raw edges of the fabric windows; as the fabric is on the bias it will create a lovely curved finish. Use the short pins to hold the folded edges in place – I pin in the same direction that I stitch, so that I do not get pricked by the pins. On the outside edge, leave the raw edges loose, or tack/baste them in place with tacking/basting thread or a glue stick. They will be covered by the binding when you finish.

8 Stitch in one direction so that you never have to twist the work round. Using the 12wt thread, make a running stitch through all of the layers to hold the bias edge down, securing the window fabric at the same time. Rubber thimbles help here to pull the needle through all the layers. Make a couple of over-sewing stitches at the point of the windows to hold everything neatly in place.

9 Stitch along each row until the work is complete. You can now bind the mini quilt. I used the completely machined method on page 25, but instead of topstitching on the machine, I have used big stitch running stitch.

MEASUREMENTS

Mini quilt size: 25½in (65cm) square

REQUIREMENTS

Base fabric: Four squares, 16½ x 16½in (42 x 42cm)

Window fabric: Eight 5in (13cm) squares; cut four of these into HST for the outside edges

Binding: Cut two 2½in (6.5cm) by WoF strips and join with bias joins. Press in half along the length, WS together

Notions: Short appliqué pins

12wt thread for hand stitching

No.6 betweens needle

Optional: a flexible rubber thimble

Tacking/basting thread or fabric glue stick

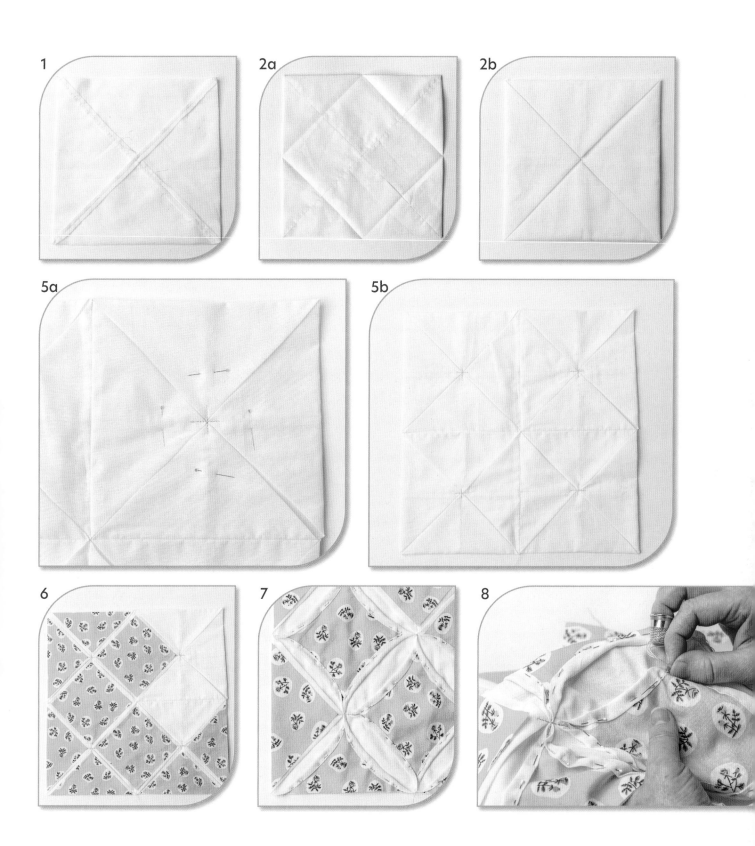

TURNING THE BLOCKS INTO A QUILT

1 Follow steps 1-2 on pages 94-95 to make 36 base blocks with flappy triangles.

2 Stitch these together into six rows of six, keeping the triangular flaps folded towards the centre as you do so.

3 Stitch two rows together to enable you to start making the windows. Stitch down the flaps on the first row (as in step 5 on page 94). You will need to keep the flaps free in the next row in order to be able to add the third row.

4 Fold over the bias fabric, then pin and stitch the triangles along the outside edge. Now stitch the second row of windows (square) in the same way. And then the third.

5 At this point you can add the third row of base squares. Then stitch down the points and start to add a fourth row of windows.

6 Remember that you are always working on the unfinished edge closest to you, and that you are only ever sewing in one direction. Build the quilt up in this way until the sixth row of base squares is complete and all the windows added. To stabilize the outside edges and cover the raw edges of the fabric, bind the quilt using one of the methods on pages 20-25.

MEASUREMENTS

Quilt size: 48in (122cm) square

Block size: 8in (20.5cm) square

REQUIREMENTS

Base fabric: 297in (7.6m) by WoF

Windows, plain green: 25in (65cm) by WoF

Windows, green print: 25in (65cm) by WoF

Binding: 12½in (35cm) by WoF

Notions: Short appliqué pins

12wt thread for hand stitching

No.6 betweens needle

Optional: a flexible rubber thimble

Tacking/basting thread OR fabric glue stick

FABRIC CUTTING

Base fabric: Cut thirty-six squares, 16½ x 16½in (42 x 42cm)

Windows, plain green: Cut five 5in (13cm) strips by WoF. Sub-cut thirty-six 5in (13cm) squares; cut six of these into HST

Windows, green print: Cut five 5in (13cm) strips by WoF. Sub-cut thirty-six 5in (13cm) squares; cut six of these into HST

Binding: Cut five strips, 2½in (6.5cm) by WoF. Join to a continuous length with bias joins, fold along the length WS together and press

9 Siddi quilting

Siddi, or Kawandi, quilts come from the western part of India, below Pakistan, and are made by people of African descent who came to India through enslavement by the Portuguese in the 16th century. These Siddi people live in North Karnatuka, and each tribe is said to make quilts with their own style and characteristics.

One of the traditions that has continued is the making of bed quilts, to be slept on in the hot weather, or under in the cooler monsoon season. They are made from a sari base and appliquéd patches of fabric are built up on top, from the outside edges working towards the centre. These patches are held down with running stitch, and the layers of overlapping patches built up to cover the base cloth. Traditionally they are finished with a folded fabric square at each corner, known as a *phula* or flower, and some consider the Kawandi unfinished or undressed without them.

An interesting fact about these quilts is that traditionally a few grains of rice will be placed under the central patch, or at the stomach/belly of the quilt, before being stitched down. There are said to be a couple of reasons for this. One is that as the quilt has been nurtured (made), it needs to be fed to ensure it will last a long time. The other is that the inclusion of the rice is to honour the Goddess Annapurna (the Goddess of Plenty) so that the user will be blessed with a full stomach.

This qualifies as a QAYG technique because you are sewing the patches to backing and lining fabrics with the quilting stitches. It is traditionally done as handwork and so is quite portable. The quilt uses small amounts of fabric or scraps, and big stitch-style quilting using a bold thread creates texture over the whole piece.

Patches of fabric have a hem folded to the WS, and then the patch is pinned onto the lined backing cloth, starting on the outside edge, or at the corners. The fabrics are then added in a circuit around the outside edge, hem folded and pinned in place as you work. Two or three rows can be placed before you start to quilt them down. The first row of stitching will keep the hem of the first circuit in place. Work all the way around the outside edge before starting on the next row of quilting. Subsequent rows of stitching are usually a finger's width apart to secure down the fabrics and the hems. The instructions given here are my interpretation of the traditional process, and may vary from other instructions given.

WORKING SIDDI PATCHWORK

1 If you are using an already hemmed backing (such as a tea towel), trim your lining fabric to fit just inside the hem. The side the hem is turned to is the WS of the backing and will be inside the quilt. Don't let the lining overlap the outside edge hem, as this will make it too bulky to stitch nicely. Place the lining on the WS of the backing and tack/baste in place.

2 If you do not have a pre-hemmed backing fabric, fold a double hem to the WS of the chosen fabric, measuring ½in (1cm) all the way around. Machine or hand-stitch in place. Now cut your lining to fit within this as in step 1 and tack/baste in place.

3 I started at all four corners with a 5in (13cm) square. But you can, in fact, start anywhere, such as the middle of one side, or at one corner, and work around. Finger press or use a seam roller here if you prefer. The corner square has two adjacent sides folded to the WS of the fabric. Use an eyeballed ¼in (5mm) as a guide. Pin the patch in place through the layers along the folded edge. Using short pins means that they won't get so caught on the thread as you work. If you want to add extra stability to the patch, use a dab of glue.

4 As you work along one side with your various sized patches, fold a hem as they overlap, so that there are no raw edges exposed. Some patches will have only one hem, and others two, three or even four. It is a very organic process. You will be deciding the size, cutting and then hemming each piece as you add it. This makes quilts made in this way unique.

5 Build up to three circuits before you start to stitch. I like to add the traditional 'flower' on each corner at this stage, as it can be secured in place with the stitching of the corner patches all in one go. I used a 2½in (6.5cm) square for each. Fold in half WS together, then fold the corners on the raw edge into the middle of the rectangle to make a triangle. Turn this triangle so that the folded side is on the back of the quilt then tuck the top of the triangle between the hemmed edges at the corner of the quilt. You will have raw edges along the long side of the triangle. Pin in place. This will be secured when you start to stitch the first line of stitches around the outside edge, keeping the hem in place.

6 Start to stitch around the folded edge of the patches using a big stitch-style running stitch, then work a circuit of stitches around the quilt top. You can hide the thread knot in the layers or leave it on top of the work depending on your preference. Secure the end of the finished thread in the same way as you would your quilting.

7 The second row and all subsequent rows of stitching are a finger's width apart. As the patches become secured you can remove the pins.

8 Continue on until you need to add more circuits of fabric – pin these in place and then continue to stitch. If some of the lines are wobbly in order to secure a hem edge, so be it; sometimes I added a single line of stitching, additional to the circuit, to secure an edge down. All of this is part of the organic nature of the work. It is often best not to think too far ahead in the layout – just work with each circuit before thinking of the next.

9 As I get closer to the centre, I begin to audition the patch that I would like to see there. The last few central patches will most likely have three if not four hemmed sides. If you do not want to put actual rice grains under the last patch, you could put some threads of fabric, use a fabric which has the look of rice, or even make stitches that look like rice grains!

Backing: I used a tea towel (loosely woven, washed and clean) as the edge is already finished and ready to work with, but you could use a piece of patchwork fabric cut to size

Lining: Thin cotton wadding/batting or cotton flannel works well, cut to the same size as your backing

Top, fabric scraps: Scraps from Jelly Rolls or yardage, as these will be cut to work on the top. The 'flowers' at each corner can be cut from one fabric or different ones. The more fabrics you use, the more interesting the quilt will be

Notions: Valdani Cotton Perle no.12, Aurifil 12wt, Wonderfil Spagetti or equivalent. I used a variegated thread but you could use solids, or different spools for a mix of colours

Tacking/basting thread

Wooden/plastic seam roller for finger pressing

Short appliqué pins

Optional: fabric glue stick

10 Once the final central patches are secured in place, your quilt is complete. Remove the tacking/basting from the back of the quilt.

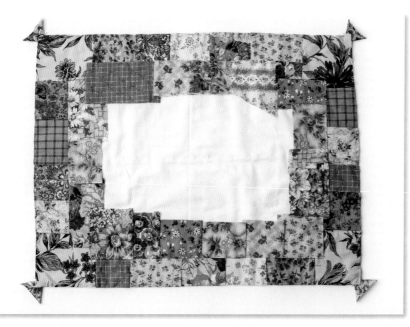

The beauty of this type of quilt is that it needs no planning. Place your fabric scraps intuitively as you go and enjoy the process.

MAKING A SIDDI PATCHWORK MINI QUILT

This small Siddi quilt is ideal for getting to grips with the method and the stitching, but alternatively you can make this quilt on a much larger scale if you prefer. Use scraps of patchwork-weight fabrics or personal cloth, labels or embroidery snippets to incorporate into your mini quilt. Simply follow the instructions given on pages 102–103. Below is a guide to how my patches were positioned, but remember that this quilting style is an organic process, and you should be guided by the fabrics you have in front of you and your own personal taste.

MEASUREMENTS

Quilt size: 19 x 25in (48.25 x 63.5cm)

REQUIREMENTS

Backing: I used a tea towel (loosely woven, washed and clean) as the edge is already finished and ready to work with, but you could use a piece of patchwork fabric cut to size

Lining: Thin cotton wadding/ batting or cotton flannel works well, cut to the same size as your backing

Top, fabric scraps: Scraps from Jelly Rolls or yardage, as these will be cut to work on the top. The 'flowers' at each corner can be cut from one fabric or different ones. The more fabrics you use, the more interesting the quilt will be

Notions: Valdani Cotton Perle no.12, Aurifil 12wt, Wonderfil Spagetti or equivalent. I used a variegated thread but you could use solids, or different spools for a mix of colours

Tacking/basting thread

Wooden/plastic seam roller for finger pressing

Short appliqué pins

Optional: fabric glue stick

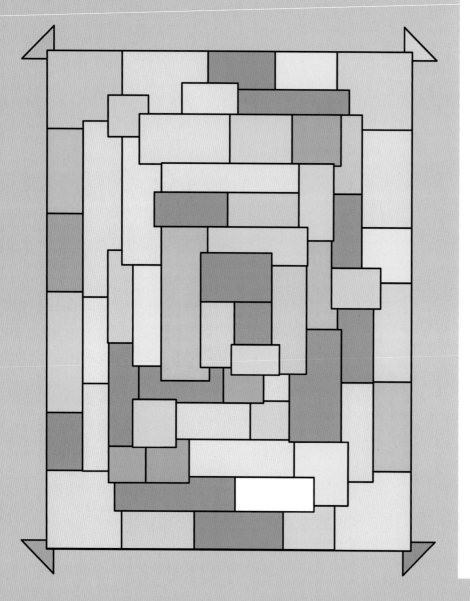

▶▶▶10 Appliqué quilting

This is a completely machine-sewn method, in which the machine quilting holds down the fabric squares. It is quick and fun, resulting in a fraying of the fabric squares, which gives an added texture to the quilt. To create the block shown opposite for use as a mini quilt, tablemat or dolly quilt, follow the instructions on pages 110–111. For more ideas and ways to develop this method further check out the Hints and Tips below, or make the complete quilt on pages 112–113. To make this as a completely machined project, choose one of the machined binding methods from pages 21–25.

MEASUREMENTS

Block size: 9 x 9in (23 x 23cm)

REQUIREMENTS

Foundation fabric: 9 x 9in (23 x 23cm)

Wadding/batting: 9½ x 9½in (24 x 24cm)

Backing: 9½ x 9½in (24 x 24cm)

Appliqué squares: Four 2½ x 2½in (6.5 x 6.5cm)

Notions: Hera marker

6 x 24in (15.25 x 61cm) rotary cutting ruler

Rotary cutting mat larger than your quilt block

Optional: spray baste

Pins, fine or short OR fabric glue stick

Machine quilting thread: I used a 35wt variegated thread

Sewing machine set up for machine quilting, with the appropriate needle

Hints and tips

▶ Make multiple blocks and use either of the machine joining techniques on pages 40-43 or 48-51 to complete a larger quilt.

▶ For more texture, layer the small squares on top of larger squares and add machine quilting lines as required.

▶ Add some big stitch hand quilting in the gaps between the squares as a contrast to the machine quilting.

▶ Add ties or buttons to the centres of the squares.

▶ Use cotton flannel for extra texture and cosiness.

▶ Bind the outer edge: the quilt on page 113 was bound using the machine-bound method on page 24.

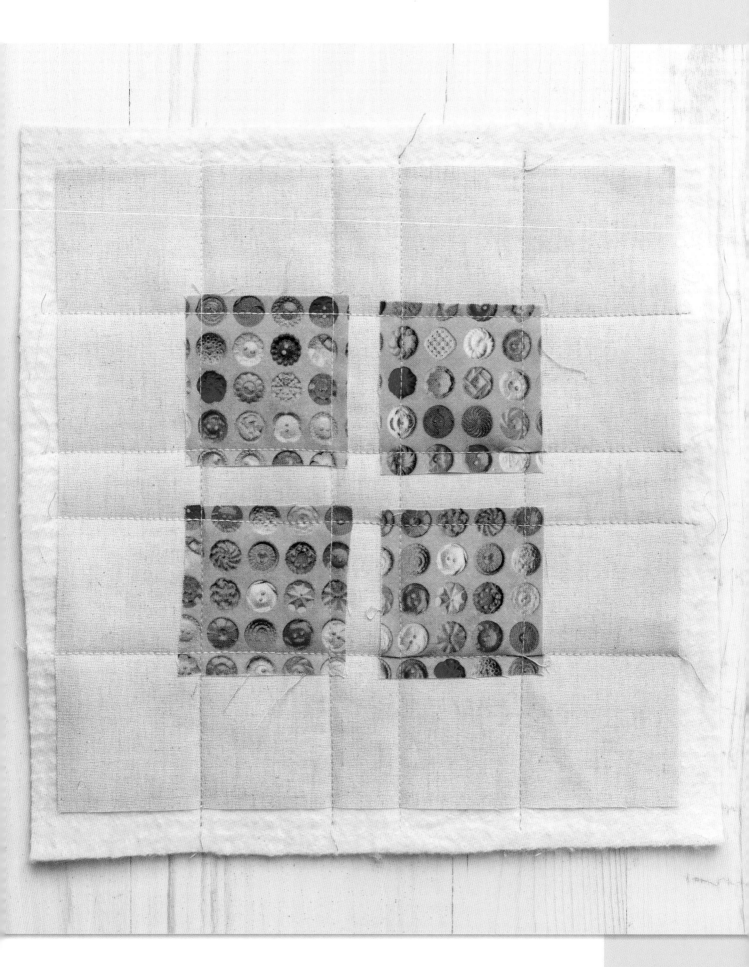

MAKING AN APPLIQUÉ QUILT BLOCK

1 Layer the backing WS up, with wadding/batting and foundation fabric RS up on top. You can use a spray baste if you like, but I find the combination of the cotton wadding/batting and the cotton fabrics tends to stick well enough without. (You can also pin the appliqué squares in place later on, as this will act as extra security.)

2 Mark out your grid on the quilt sandwich with a long rotary cutting ruler, a hera marker and the cutting mat for accuracy. Place the quilt sandwich on the cutting mat, centrally on the grid, and squared up to it. Measure from the central line on the mat running through the centre of the quilt, and score a line ½in (1cm) either side of that. This will ensure the grid is central on your block. Working in one direction, measure and mark as shown below.

3 When all the lines are complete, turn the block by 90 degrees and mark in the same way in the other direction.

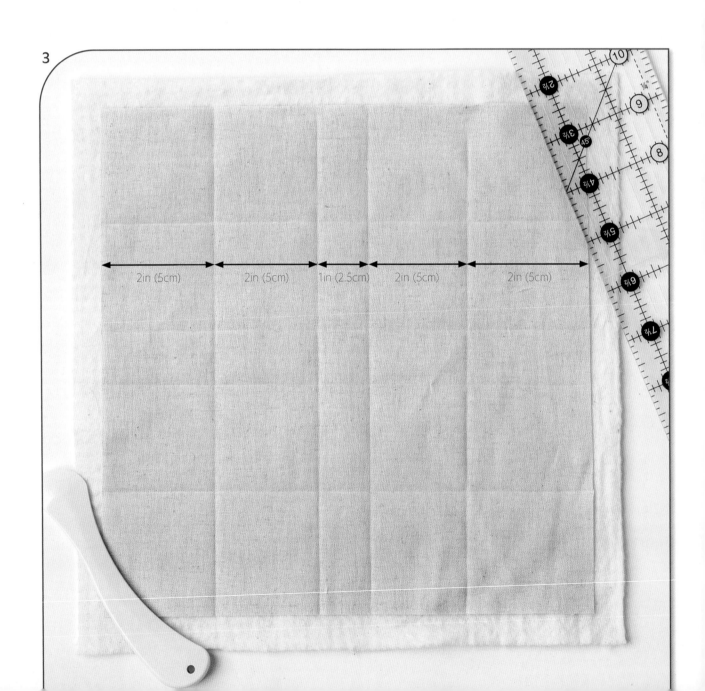

3

2in (5cm)   2in (5cm)   1in (2.5cm)   2in (5cm)   2in (5cm)

4 Now place the 2½in (6.5cm) squares on the grid, central to each 2in (5cm) square. You can see that the squares overlap the marked lines. These lines are the guide for the stitching, and the square will be about ¼in (5mm) bigger on each side – this is your SA. You can play with the patterns here, or go with a random scrappy approach. Once you are happy, either pin in place (the pin needn't go through all of the layers), or use a dab of glue stick.

5 Starting in the centre of the quilt sandwich, stitch through all of the layers on the sewing machine. This will now hold the patches in place, and you can remove the pins as you go. Stitch a central line first, then turn the quilt to stitch a central line on the next side. Keep turning the quilt and stitching outwards in this way and you will be building up a quilted grid which secures the patches.

6 Once complete, trim to 9in (23cm). You can now bind and label the mini quilt, if you wish. Once bound, the mini quilt can be washed. This will create the frayed texture. I put it in the machine on a regular wash with other laundry. Either line dry or lightly tumble to get rid of excess moisture before putting on a clothes airer. Once dry, check the fraying and tidy up the stray ends by snipping them off.

7 The quilt on pages 112–113 shows you what can be achieved by stitching multiple blocks with more appliqué squares, using the completely machine joined method and binding to finish.

4

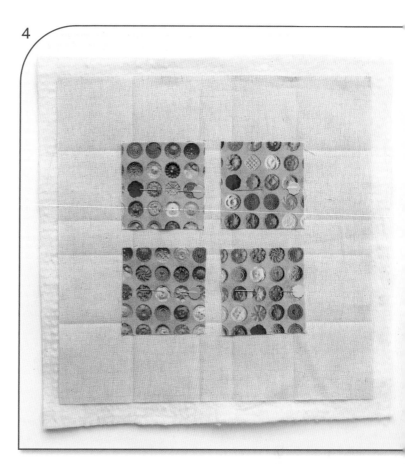

5

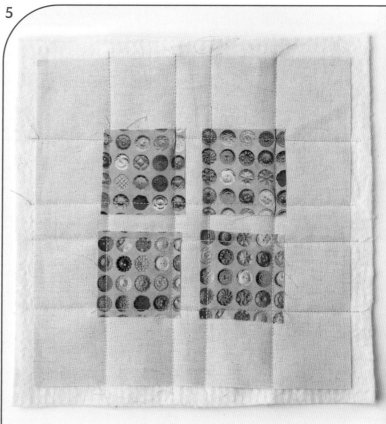

TURNING THE BLOCKS INTO A QUILT

1 Prepare and stitch nine blocks following the instructions on pages 110–111, but using 25 appliqué patches per block, rather than four. You will need to mark out your guidelines accordingly.

2 To join, I used the completely machined method on page 48.

3 I bound the quilt using the completely machined binding method on page 24.

4 To create the frayed texture, put the quilt in the washing machine, line dry and then trim the loose ends to tidy up.

MEASUREMENTS

Quilt size: 54 x 54in (138 x 138cm)

Block size: 17½ x 17½in (44.5 x 44.5cm)

REQUIREMENTS

Foundation/front of quilt: 100in (2.6m) by WoF. I used a cotton/linen mix, as I think the texture works well with this style of quilt

Appliqué squares: For a unified look: 37½in (96cm) by WoF

OR for a scrappy look: six Mini Charm packs (containing forty-two squares), which yield 252 2½in (6.5cm) squares

OR fifty-seven 5in (13cm) Charm Squares, which yield 228 2½in (6.5cm) squares

OR fifteen 2½in (6.5cm) strips by WoF, which yield 240 2½in (6.5cm) squares

OR twenty-nine 10in (25.5cm) Layer Cake squares, which yield 232 2½in (6.5cm) squares

OR five Fat Quarters (20 x 18in/51 x 45.75cm), which yield 280 2½in (6.5cm) squares

Wadding/batting: Nine 21in (54cm) squares

Backing: 105in (2.7m) by WoF

Joining strips, front: 6in (15cm) by WoF

Joining strips, back: 9½in (24cm) by WoF

Binding: 16½in (45cm) by WoF

Notions: Hera marker

Pins, fine or short, OR fabric glue stick

Machine quilting thread: I used a 35wt variegated thread

Sewing machine set up for machine quilting, with the appropriate needle

FABRIC CUTTING

Foundation/front of quilt: Cut nine 20in (51cm) squares

Appliqué squares: Cut 225 2½in (6.5cm) squares

Backing: Cut nine 21in (54cm) squares

Joining strips, front: Cut six 1in (2.5cm) by WoF strips. Remove the selvedges/selvages. Join three strips to form a continuous length, press the seams open, then sub-cut two 1 x 55in (2.5 x 140cm). Cut six 1 x 19in (2.5 x 48.25cm) pieces from the remaining strips

Joining strips, back: Cut six 1½in (4cm) by WoF strips. Remove the selvedges/selvages. Join three strips to form a continuous length, press the seams open and sub-cut two 1½ x 55in (4 x 140cm) strips. Cut six 1½ x 19in (4 x 48.25cm) pieces from the remaining strips

Binding: Cut six 2¾in (7cm) by WoF strips. Join to a continuous length, with bias joins, removing the selvedges/selvages. Press WS together along the length

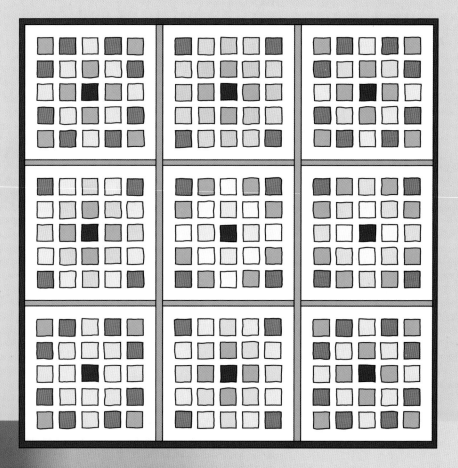

▶▶ 11 Lined circles

This method of making a quilt or coverlet (depending on whether you include a thin layer of wadding/batting within each circle or not), simply consists of sewing fabric circles RS together, turning them RS out, marking them into squares, then sewing straight seams to stitch them together.

The effect is like that of an Orange Peel patchwork quilt, but without any of the fiddly piecing of curves. Once the circles are sewn and turned RS out they need to be marked with straight lines, making a square. You can do this by marking around the template with a Hera marker or by making a heat-proof template (such as Mylar) and pressing. Alternatively, cut thin card and cover it in tin foil and use this to press the square. Look out for rotary cutting circle templates, as this will also make things quicker if used with a turntable cutting mat.

This is a nice technique, as you work on the front and back of the quilt at the same time. It also requires no binding, as I like to leave the outside edges scalloped. Take note of the instructions when it comes to hand-sewing or machine-sewing the flaps down – the order for each is slightly different, in both cases to make the process easier for that particular method. Once you've tried out the method on pages 116–117, experiment with further ideas, using different fabric and colour combinations.

FURTHER IDEAS

▸ Stitch the fabric circles WS together (so no turning though). Stitch together as shown on pages 116–117, and stitch down the flaps. When you sew this version, you end up with textured, frayed edges.

▸ Use old denim jeans or upholstery-weight fabrics for a heavier, very durable quilt.

▸ Use just two fabrics, one for the back and one for the front. For the quilt shown on pages 118–119 you'll need 180in (4.6m) by WoF of Fabric A, and 180in (4.6m) by WoF of Fabric B. Cut eighteen 10in (25.5cm) by WoF strips from each fabric. Sub-cut into 10in (25.5cm) squares. This makes it easier to handle cutting circles as opposed to grappling with yardage.

▸ Include a thin wadding/batting or cotton flannel fabric when layering and stitching to add extra bulk. Layer this next to the WS of one fabric circle before stitching.

▸ Stitch the flaps down by hand with an appliqué stitch, buttonhole stitch or herringbone stitch.

▸ Fussy-cut the circles to feature a motif in the centre for a fun I-Spy quilt for children.

MAKING A LINED CIRCLES MINI QUILT

1 Pair up the circles RS together. It works well if you have circles that contrast when paired up, as when one fabric is folded over to the other, the curved shape is then shown off nicely. I try to line up the straight of grain, as it can make for a more stable seam (as in future steps you will match up the square template to the straight of grain). Stitch on the machine, using a ¼in (5mm) SA. Simply stitch all the way round, and overlap the stitches by 1in (2.5cm) to finish, then snip the thread.

2 You now need to make a small slit in one of the circles. It will need to be on the side that will be folded over, as this will hide the slit. It needs to be about 2in (5cm) long, and close to the fold line of the square. Use your square template to show you where the lines will sit. If you want to, you could mark the lines of the square with pencil for guidance to start with, but after a few you will be able to gauge where to cut.

3 Turn through to the RS by drawing the edge furthest from the slit through first; the rest will easily follow. Use a wooden chopstick or wooden seam creaser to push out the seam edge. Personally, I really like the chopstick, as it is longer and easier to reach all of the circle. Once done, the circle can be lightly pressed.

4 Now press or mark the square onto the side of the circle that will be the front of the quilt using a Hera marker, if you have one. I try to line the square up with the straight of grain.

5 You can decide on a layout for the circles, or randomly select and pair them up for stitching. You will be creating two rows of two circles. Hold two lined circles back sides together and line up the creased squares. When making the rows, I tend to try to incorporate the slit edge in these seams. Pin perpendicular to the straight crease and stitch along this, securing the stitches with backstitch at each end of the seam.

6 Repeat for the second row.

7 If you are hand-stitching the flaps down, I would do this now on each row, before joining it to the next. If you are machining, you need to wait.

8 Now stitch the rows to each other. Pin at the seam joins, or use fabric clips, as these don't distort when there may be bulky seams.

9 If you are machine stitching the flaps down you can now do this along the row you have just sewn. Start at one end and stitch along the edge of the flap, alternating to the other side of the seam at the junction. You will end up having sewn an undulating line, and half of the flaps down. With the needle still in the work, lift the presser foot, turn the work round and go back up the seam, sewing down the remaining flaps. Doing it this way means there are less ends of thread to stitch in.

MEASUREMENTS

Mini quilt size: 15 x 15in (38 x 38cm)

REQUIREMENTS

Circles: Eight 10in (25.5cm) squares

Notions: Circle template (see page 142)

Square template (see page 140)

Optional: Hera marker

Machine quilting thread

Wooden chopstick or seam creaser

Sewing machine thread to tone with the circles for stitching

Optional: fabric clips

Optional: heat-resistant template plastic (such as Mylar) or thin card wrapped in tin foil

FABRIC CUTTING

Circles: Cut eight circles 9½in (24cm) in diameter using the template

1

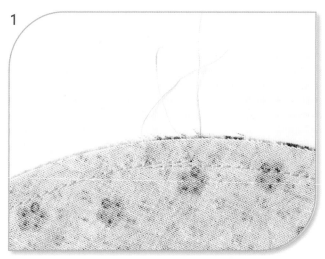

2

3

4

5

8

9

TURNING THE LINED CIRCLES INTO A QUILT

1 Pair up the circles, RS together. This quilt works well if you have circles that contrast paired up, as when one fabric is folded over to the other, the curved shape is then shown off nicely. Follow steps 1 to 4 on page 116 to make up 72 lined circles.

2 You can decide on a layout for the circles, or randomly select and pair them up for stitching. You will be creating nine rows of eight circles.

3 Hold two lined circles back sides together and line up the creased squares. When making the rows, I tend to try to incorporate the slit edge in these seams. Pin perpendicular to the straight crease and stitch along this, securing the stitches with backstitch at each end of the seam.

4 Continue along the row, joining eight circles to each other. You can pin the flaps down as you work to stop them getting in the way. Make nine rows in the same way.

5 If you are hand-stitching the flaps down, I would do this now on each row, before joining it to the next. If you are machining, you need to wait.

6 Now stitch the rows together. Pin at the seam joins, or use fabric clips, as these don't distort when there may be bulky seams. Join the first two rows together.

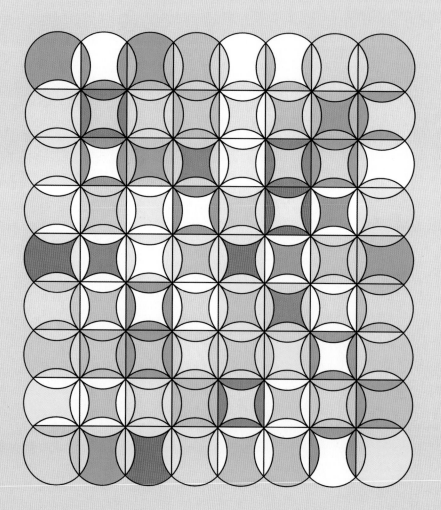

MEASUREMENTS

Quilt size: 51 x 58½in (130 x 148.5cm)

REQUIREMENTS

Circles: You can use pre-cut Layer Cakes (10in/25.5cm squares) for a scrappy look; four Layer Cakes will be enough for the whole quilt

If you want to use one consistent fabric for the front AND/OR the back, then 180in (4.6m) by WoF of each will yield seventy-two circles. You can combine this with the scrappy circles depending on the look, or use two consistent fabrics throughout (see Further Ideas, page 114)

Notions: Circle template (see page 142)

Square template (see page 140)

Optional: Hera marker

Machine quilting thread

Wooden chopstick or seam creaser

Sewing-machine thread to tone with the circles for stitching

Optional: fabric clips

Optional: heat-resistant template plastic (such as Mylar) or thin card wrapped in tin foil

FABRIC CUTTING

Circles: Cut 144 circles (9½in/24cm diameter), using the template: seventy-two for the front and seventy-two for the back

7 If you are machine-stitching the flaps down you can now do this along the row you have just sewn. Start at one end and stitch along the edge of the flap, alternating to the other side of the seam at each junction. You will end up having sewn an undulating line, and half of the flaps down. With the needle still in the work, lift the presser foot, turn the work round and go back up the seam, sewing down the remaining flaps. Doing it this way means there are less ends of thread to stitch in on every row.

8 Now add the third row and repeat to stitch the flaps down.

9 To make it easier to handle the rows, now sew rows 4 and 5 and 6 together, then quilt.

10 Then sew together rows 7, 8 and 9.

11 Now sew the three sections together, quilting along the flaps on each new seam you make. The quilt now needs to have the remaining flaps stitched down if you are working by machine. Again, work along the seams, up and down as before, stitching in the thread ends to complete.

▶▶ 12 Fringed quilting

The patches of this quilt are individually machine quilted with the backing and lining before being stitched into a quilt. This method works well for a fun snuggle quilt – for something with some texture – and it gives the appearance of being like a Candlewick bedspread.

This simple QAYG method works really well with cotton flannel or brushed cotton fabrics, as the texture of the frayed edges gives the finished quilt a lovely snuggly appearance. But equally, you could also use patchwork cotton for the front and the back.

The quilt is stitched and quilted on the sewing machine, does not need pressing as you work, and does not need a binding. All of these things make it a speedy and fun method. The snipped or fringed edges, once washed when the quilt is complete, will fray slightly and give a wonderful soft appearance.

Use a neutral thread for the machine quilting if you don't want it to be so bold, or use a contrast thread for some definition. Play around with the stitch length – I usually like a longer than normal stitch. You could even use some decorative machine stitches for added fun.

The finished blocks unwashed (above, opposite), and washed and softened (below and below, opposite).

MAKING A FRINGED 4-BLOCK MINI QUILT

1 Layer up the backing square, WS up, then the lining and then front RS up. These do not usually need pinning or tacking/basting, as the cotton fabrics tend to stick to each other, and it is only a small area to be quilted so will hold flat.

2 You can mark the diagonal lines on the front fabric with a Hera marker and ruler. You will probably find that once you have done this for a few squares, and quilted them, your eye will be 'in', and there is no need to keep marking them.

3 On the sewing machine, using the 28wt thread on the spool and 40wt in the bobbin, stitch the diagonals, quilting the three layers together. If you prepare these all ahead of time, then you can chain quilt them, speeding up the process. Simply quilt them all in one direction, snip the threads, then quilt in the second direction. Once the layered squares are quilted you are ready to stitch them together.

4 Stitch them into pairs using 50wt thread in the machine top and bobbin. Stitch from raw edge to raw edge with a ½in (1cm) SA, with the squares WS together - the seam will be on the front of the quilt.

5 Once the pairs are stitched, you will need to snip into the SA. Leave about 1in (2.5cm) unsnipped at each end of the seam, as this will then be stitched into the next seam. If you cut too close to either end, the new seam might not be as stable as it should be. The snips are about ¼in (5mm) apart; snip through all six layers to within ⅛in (3mm) of the seam stitches.

6 Stitch two pairs together, to make a four-patch block. Make sure the SA are facing in opposite directions at the junction, so they knit together, and the bulk is evenly distributed. Stitch from raw edge to raw edge and then snip the SA as before.

7 To secure the outside edge of the mini quilt, machine all the way round the outside edge, ½in (1cm) from the edge. Do this twice. It does not matter if the lines are not identical. You can snip the edge, too, if you like, or leave it as it is.

8 Once this is done, you can wash the quilt in the washing machine. I used my usual washing soap and put it in for a quick wash and full spin. Once out, you can tumble dry it to get some of the excess moisture out then put it on a radiator, or on the line dry on a windy day. Either way, the quilt will end up with a lovely worn and textured look.

REQUIREMENTS

Front: Four 5in (13cm) squares. I used woven flannel fabrics, but printed or plain coloured flannel will work equally well

Backing: Four 5in (13cm) squares. I used a woven check here, not a flannel, but you can use either, or a printed cotton, too

Lining: Four 5in (13cm) squares of cotton flannel. Use a plain white or cream inexpensive fabric, as this will be mostly hidden in the quilt. The edges will show in the fringing only. Using a woven fabric in the lining means that it will fray in the same way as the outer fabrics, whereas a wadding/batting will not

Notions: Hera marker and ruler to mark diagonal lines

Machine quilting thread: I used 28wt on the spool and 40wt in the bobbin, with a size 90 machine needle; I used 50wt thread to stitch the quilt squares together

Sharp scissors for snipping the edges: I used Merchant and Mills Buttonhole scissors

3

4

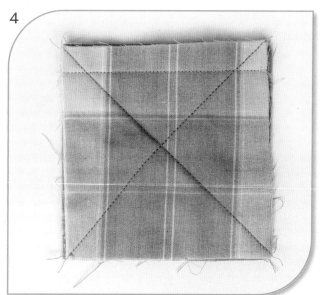

5

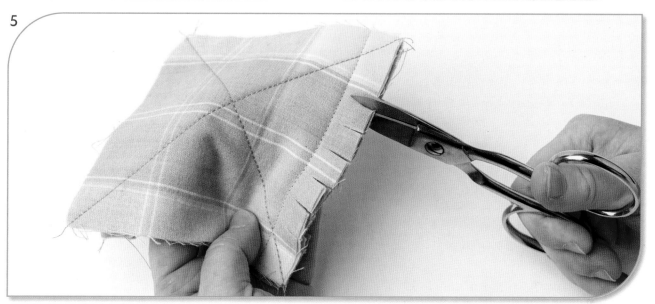

7

TURNING THE BLOCKS INTO A QUILT

1 Following steps 1 to 6 on pages 122–123, make up thirty-six four-patch blocks. This quilt consists of six rows of six four-patch blocks. Once all of the four-patch blocks are sewn and snipped they can be stitched into rows.

2 When joining the blocks to make the rows, alternate the direction of the long seam in each block and knit the junction seams. If it helps, use a pin perpendicular to the raw edge each side of the seam to keep it in place, or use fabric clips.

3 Once each row is sewn, snip into the SA.

4 Join the rows together, in the same way, alternating the direction of the seams at the junctions. Snip the seams as each row is sewn.

5 Once all of the rows are complete, and snipped, finish off the outside edge of the quilt. This is done by stitching all the way around the outside edge with two rows of stitching ½in (1cm) from the raw edge. Start and stop on each side at the raw edge. I try to get the lines close to each other, but not on top of each other. I use the 28wt thread that I used for the quilting here. I stitch the SA on the outside edge down in the same direction as the seam in the quilt. Once complete, snip the outside edge.

6 Once this is done you can wash the quilt as described in step 7 on page 122.

MEASUREMENTS

Quilt size: 49in (125cm) square

REQUIREMENTS

Front: 90in (2.3m) by WoF cut into 144 5in (13cm) squares. I used woven flannel fabrics, but printed or plain coloured flannel would work equally well. I made a scrappy top for this quilt. To achieve a similar effect, it is helpful to know the yield of some pre-cuts, as this allows you to buy lots of different prints without buying more yardage than you might need:

one 5in (13cm) by WoF strip yields eight 5in (13cm) squares

four Charm Packs yield 168 5in (13cm) squares

two Layer Cakes yield 168 5in (13cm) squares

one Fat Quarter yields twelve 5in (13cm) squares; twelve Fat Quarters yield 144 5in (13cm) squares

Alternatively, use your stash, as this is a great way to use up fabrics

Backing: 90in (2.3m) by WoF cut into 144 5in (13cm) squares. I used a woven check here, not a flannel, but you can use that or printed cotton too. You can make the back scrappy like the front, but I chose to use a single fabric

Lining: 90in (2.3m) by WoF cut into 144 5in (13cm) squares. I used a cotton flannel – use a plain white or cream inexpensive fabric, as this will be mostly hidden in the quilt. The edges will show in the fringing only. Using a woven fabric in the lining means that it will fray in the same way as the outer fabrics, whereas a wadding/batting will not

Notions: Hera marker and ruler to mark diagonal lines

Machine quilting thread: I used 28wt on the spool and 40wt in the bobbin, with a size 90 machine needle; I used 50wt thread to stitch the quilt squares together

Sharp scissors for snipping the edges: I used Merchant and Mills Buttonhole scissors

Optional: fabric clips

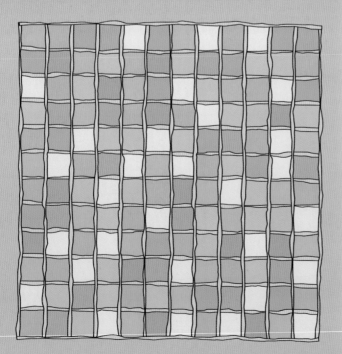

This patchwork consists of many self-lined gathered fabric circles. They are made and stitched together by hand to form all-over designs or purely random scrappy-style coverlets. The circles have no wadding/batting (hence they form a coverlet rather than a quilt), but the gathering gives them a textured, quilty look. The small amount of fabric needed to make each puff and the ease of the hand stitching makes it a popular and portable project.

This type of patchwork was seen initially in the 1920s, but it was not until later on that it gained popularity and was seen in various women's periodicals. Many of the examples that come up for sale as vintage pieces are placed around the 1930s, and contain lovely examples for fabric prints from that time. These types of quilts became popular in the 1930s and 1940s in the US, and in the 1970s McCalls published popular patterns using the puff for toys. In the US it became known as Yo Yo patchwork, as its shape is similar to that of the Yo Yo toy that was introduced in the 1920s.

In the UK, the patchwork is referred to as Suffolk puff patchwork. It is thought to have originated in Suffolk, hence the name, and mentions of it go back to 1601. It is thought that the circles, then made and stuffed with wool by the rural community, were then stitched together as quilts. Over the years the wool stuffing has been forgotten, and the circles make a light patchwork throw with a lacy effect.

Fabric options:

Fabrics commonly used are lightweight patchwork or dressmaking cottons, but you may also want to try out soft double gauze, crepe, Tana lawn or lightweight linen.

Threads:

Use a strong thread to stitch around the hemmed circle, as it needs to be drawn up and sewn in place. I use 28wt for this and for stitching the patches together. Try to use a muted tone that you can use throughout the project to avoid chopping and changing.

Needles:

Use a sharps size 10, or whatever you are comfortable with.

Templates:

Any circle can be used to cut the fabric. Find a household object, draw around it on the fabric, right or wrong side, cut it out and you are ready. Alternatively, make a template from thick card or template plastic, or look for acrylic template circles that allow you to rotary cut the circles. This works really well with the use of a turntable cutting mat. Depending on the finished size of the puff you want, start with a circle about two and a half times bigger.

Specialist Yo Yo makers:

Clover® makes a special disc set that allows you to sandwich a square of fabric between two circles, trim, and then stitch to a regulated stitch length, remove and gather. This is the method I used to make the project coverlet (see opposite and on pages 130–131).

Planning your layout:

You might want to plan your design and create something quite organized with your use of colours, laying them out in all number of designs. Generally the circles are sewn together in rows, leaving a diamond shape gap between the circles. You can stagger the rows, or stitch the circles together into a flower/hexagon shape, and this leaves smaller triangular gaps between the circles. You might also want to use different sizes together in the same project. This looks most effective when used as an edging to the coverlet.

Hints and tips:

- You can appliqué all of the lacy patchwork on to a base fabric if you want a heavier coverlet.
- Generally, each puff is made from one fabric, but fabrics can be pieced and then cut into circles, creating more complex design options.
- You can create designs by arranging the colours and patterns of the fabric in specific ways.
- Using different size puffs can create an edging on the patchwork, as this technique does not require binding.

Making puffs the traditional way

Cut your fabric circle and prepare your thread as in steps 1–2 opposite. Fold a narrow hem (a scant ¼in/5mm), to the WS of the fabric, and with the knotted thread start sewing a running stitch, as you fold the edge over. Use stitches about ¼in (5mm) long and about ⅛in (3mm) in from the fold. You do not need to be too exact, but I think you get a nicer finish if you don't sew right on the edge of the fold. Gather the thread gently, then oversew as in step 6, opposite, to secure your puff.

MAKING SUFFOLK PUFFS USING A YO YO MAKER

1 Cut a circle of fabric using the 5in (13cm) template; the finished size will be 2½in (6.5cm) diameter. Place it on top of the backing disc, RS down, then push the upper disc on top to secure it, making sure the fabric is central and that the holes in the two discs line up, and the balance dots.

2 Thread a needle with thread long enough to go all the way around the outside edge of the circle with some to spare. Tie a good knot at the end as you do not want this to pull through when you gather up the fabric. You want to be using a matching or toning thread so that it doesn't show up so much.

3 Use the guide holes on the discs to create neat, even running stitches around the edge of your fabric. When you get back to the start, stitch one stitch past the knot, leaving the thread to come up on the RS of the fabric. Remember that the stitches travel along the gap on the back of the template. If not you will stitch the template to the fabric.

4 Slip the backing disc off, as shown.

5 Gently remove the upper disc. Now gently pull the thread to create the gathers. This gathered side is seen as the RS or front of the patchwork.

6 When complete, oversew in one place to secure the thread, and snip. If you want a more secure finish, work backstitch in a circle, just catching the gathers, on the back of the puff, and secure with a couple of stitches on top of each other.

7 The finished puff.

8 When joining the puffs, hold two together with the gathered sides facing. Start with a small knot in the thread and come up from the inside of the puff. Make a small oversewing or whip stitch to catch the edge of the folds together. At most you will sew along ½in (1cm), before turning and going back over the stitches. You do not want to distort the shape of the circle by sewing too far. Finish the thread with a couple of stitches on top of each other and you can thread the needle back through the inside of the puff before snipping.

1 Make 12 puffs from one fabric.

2 Join the puffs together into pairs.

3 Join the pairs into blocks of fours. You might find it useful to pin the puffs together. I usually secure the ones I am not stitching to keep them stable with a fabric clip. This keeps things in place but does not distort the shapes. Once the first puffs are joined, remove the clip ready to sew the second pair. You will make three blocks of four from each fabric.

4 Make 80 of these four-patch units (there will be four spare).

5 Join the units together to create ten rows of eight units. Use clips to keep things stable as you work. I did this quite randomly, and then organized them into the whole throw.

6 Organize the rows so you are happy with the placement.

7 Clip two rows together, and stitch.

8 Continue until the coverlet is complete.

MEASUREMENTS

Quilt size: 44 x 35in (112 x 89cm)

REQUIREMENTS

Fabric: Twenty-seven different fabrics, each 11in (28cm) by WoF. I used a double gauze fabric, which is soft to handle and gathers up nicely. I wanted to make a scrappy-style throw, but did not want the impact of the fabric prints I had chosen to get lost in the patchwork. For this reason I stitched the same prints into units of four, but randomly placed them around the throw. When cutting my fabrics, I find it easier to cut squares, then use these to cut the circles from. You can, of course, cut circles from your yardage, without cutting squares first if you like

Notions: Circle template, 5in (13cm) diameter (see page 140)

Pins and fabric clips

FABRIC CUTTING

Fabric: From each fabric cut two strips, 5½in (13cm) by WoF. Sub-cut to twelve 5½in (13cm) squares. Cut your circles from these fabric squares using the template

▶▶ 14 Pojabi patchwork

Also known as 'Bojabi', this traditional form of Korean patchwork is characteristically made from a sheer, stiff organza-type fabric and stitched by hand. The method of stitching creates an enclosed seam, so the work is double-sided. Smaller pieces can be used as wrapping cloths for gift giving, and larger pieces work well as window dressings. The patchwork takes on a stained-glass effect due to the dense seams and the sheer fabrics.

The seaming method used for Pojabi patchwork has always reminded me of a seam used in garment making called a run-and-fell seam (sometimes know as a flat-felled seam, or a lapped seam when viewed from the WS). Due to this, I saw it as a quick and easy way to stitch the patchwork by machine, by hand, or a combination of both.

This style of patchwork fits neatly into the QAYG family, as the patchwork you are stitching is finished neatly with the seaming method whether by hand or machine. By sewing on the machine, the patchwork can incorporate any weight of fabric, so that you can make a patchwork throw or coverlet (as there is no wadding/batting) as well as the customary wrapping cloth or window dressing. The stitched and finished seams create a slight texture and the visible sewing lines are reminiscent of machine quilting.

Wrapping cloths made of lightweight fabrics like Tana lawn or double gauze look lovely and are easily stitched by hand. Something larger like a window dressing could even incorporate some Broderie Anglaise. Heavier fabrics like denim or barkcloth would make a fun picnic throw or decorative patchwork coverlet. Experiment with the methods and fabrics to see how versatile this QAYG method can be.

After playing with sewing threads, I concluded that stitching all the methods in a 28wt thread on the spool and the bobbin gave the best result. You achieve a bold, durable stitch which works for both hand and machine sewing. When machining, remember to choose a larger needle size for the thread.

MACHINE-ONLY METHOD

1

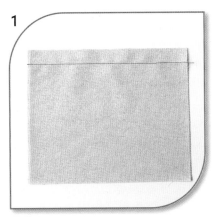

2

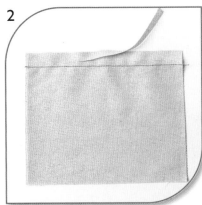

3

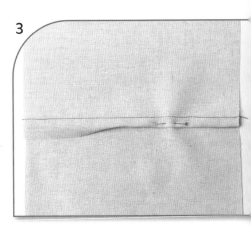

1 Place two strips of fabric RS together. Using a ¾in (2cm) SA stitch them together.

2 Trim one SA back to about ¼in (5mm).

3 Now press from the RS, laying the fabrics so that the larger SA covers the trimmed one. By doing this from the front/RS of the work you never press in a crease (that can happen if you press from the WS), which then needs a second pressing to remove. Turn the work to the WS so that you can see the SA, then fold the larger SA in half, enclosing the trimmed SA. Press as you fold and pin.

4 On the sewing machine, stitch along the folded edge of the SA.

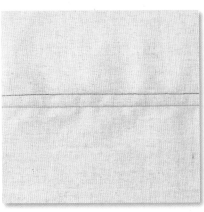

From the front.

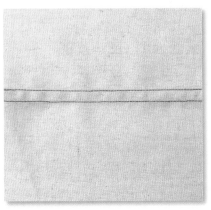

From the back.

HAND-ONLY METHOD

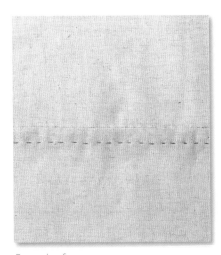

From the front.

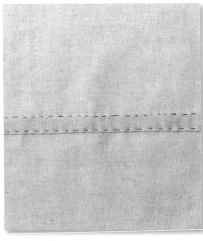

From the back.

1 On the WS of one of the fabric pieces draw a line with a fabric pencil or crease with a Hera marker ¾in (2cm) from the raw edge.

2 Pair up your fabrics as in step 1 of the machine-only method above and, starting with knotted thread and a backstitch, stitch with a small running stitch along the line. Secure as above.

3 Cut, press and finish as in steps 2 and 3 for the machine-only method, then complete the stitching by hand.

MACHINE AND HAND METHOD

1 Follow steps 1–3 of the machine-only method, opposite, to stitch and fold your fabric SA.

2 Starting with a knotted thread, hand stitch a small running stitch to hold down the folded edge. To finish, secure with a couple of backstitches.

3 From the WS you can see both the machined line and the hand-stitched line; from the front you can see the hand-stitched line only.

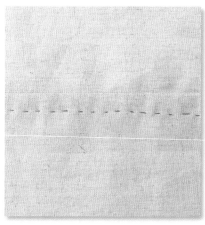

From the front.

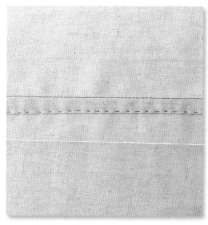

From the back.

CREATING A BLOCK

1

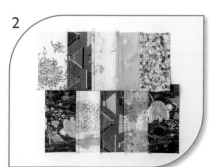

2

4

5

1 Using your chosen method (hand, hand and machine or machine-only), join together five fabric strips into a row. Repeat with a second set of five, as shown.

2 You need to offset the seams, as shown. Place the two strips RS together and sew together with a ¾in (2cm) seam.

3 Trim one of the SA back to about ¼in (5mm).

4 Now press from the RS, laying the fabrics so that the larger SA covers the trimmed one. Turn the work to the WS so that you can see the SA, and fold the larger SA in half, enclosing the trimmed SA. Press as you fold and pin.

5 On the sewing machine, stitch along the folded edge of the SA.

6 Trim the block square.

6

MAKING A POJABI QUILT

This lightweight patchwork works beautifully as a window drape (shown on pages 138–139), or equally well as a throw on the sofa.

1 Place two strips of fabric RS together.

2 Using a ¾in (2cm) SA, stitch them together.

3 Trim one SA to about ¼in (5mm).

4 Now press from the RS, laying the fabrics so that the larger SA covers the trimmed one.

5 Turn the work to the WS so that you can see the SA, then fold the larger SA in half, enclosing the trimmed SA. Press as you fold and pin.

6 On the sewing machine, stitch along the folded edge of the SA.

7 Complete all 28 of the fabric pairs in the same way.

8 Cut each strip into two 8½in (21.5cm) sections: 56 in total.

9 Pair up these sections for stitching, mixing the fabrics up as you go. Check that the direction of the finished seams all go the same way. Make 28.

MEASUREMENTS

Quilt size: 45½ x 49in (116 x 125cm)

REQUIREMENTS

Fabric: Twenty-eight different fabrics, each 4½in (11.5cm) by WoF

Notions: 28wt sewing thread in the bobbin and on the spool

Hera marker

FABRIC CUTTING

Fabric: Cut each strip in half creating fifty-six strips, each 4½in (11.5cm) deep. This allows for the maximum combination of fabrics even though you will be sewing then cutting for ease of construction. If you prefer, you can keep the strips WoF, which will result in more repeated combinations

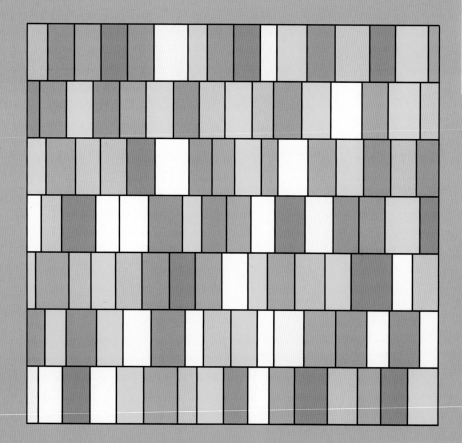

10 Stitch the pairs together to make strips of four fabrics – when you trim to make the seam finish, make sure you trim to allow the folded seams to all go in the same direction.

11 Stitch four of these strips of four fabrics together to create one row, again, checking on the seam direction.

12 Make seven rows in the same way.

13 Arrange the rows and stagger them slightly at each end so that each SA falls roughly in the middle of each fabric, in a brick-like pattern; ensure all of the seam finishes go in the same direction.

14 Stitch each row together following the same seaming method.

15 Trim the excess fabric from the edges of the quilt to make the sides straight.

16 Once complete, finish off the outside edges. Turn under a double ⅜in (1cm) hem.

TEMPLATES

All of the templates shown on pages 140–143 are reproduced actual size. Simply copy them onto firm card or template plastic and cut neatly around the outline.

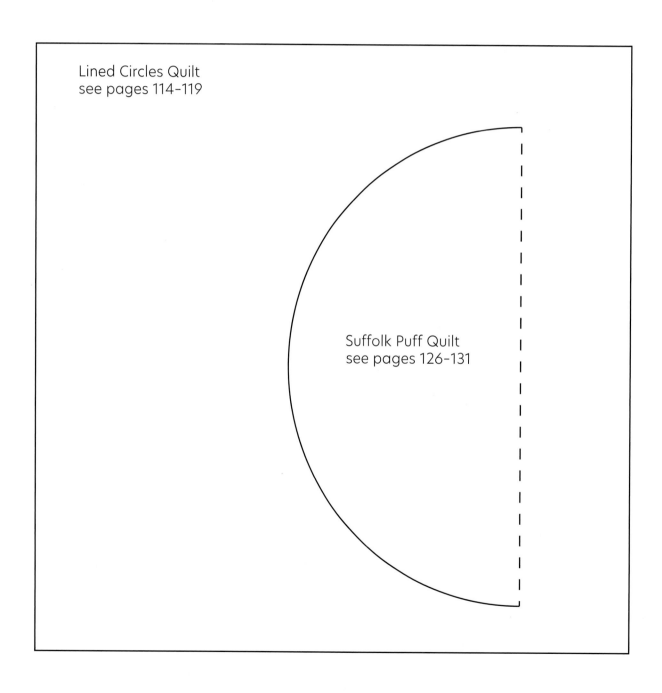

Lined Circles Quilt
see pages 114–119

Suffolk Puff Quilt
see pages 126–131

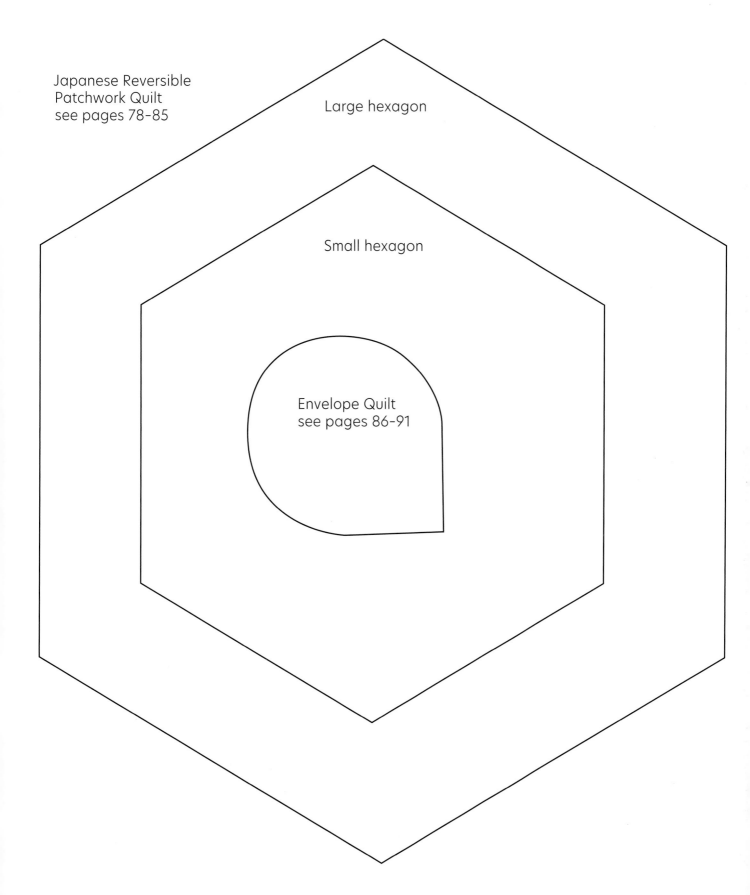

Japanese Reversible
Patchwork Quilt
see pages 78-85

Large hexagon

Small hexagon

Envelope Quilt
see pages 86-91

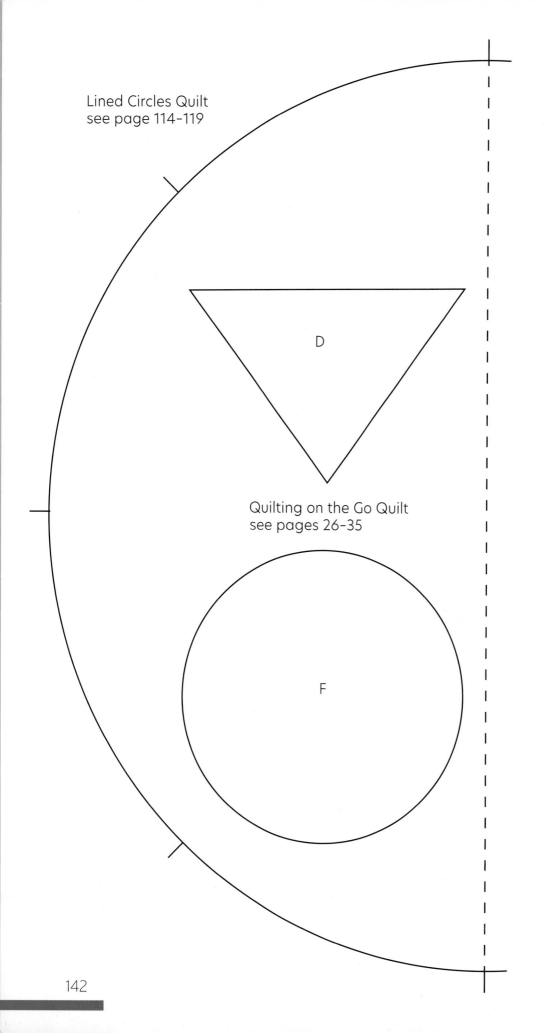

Lined Circles Quilt
see page 114–119

D

Quilting on the Go Quilt
see pages 26–35

F

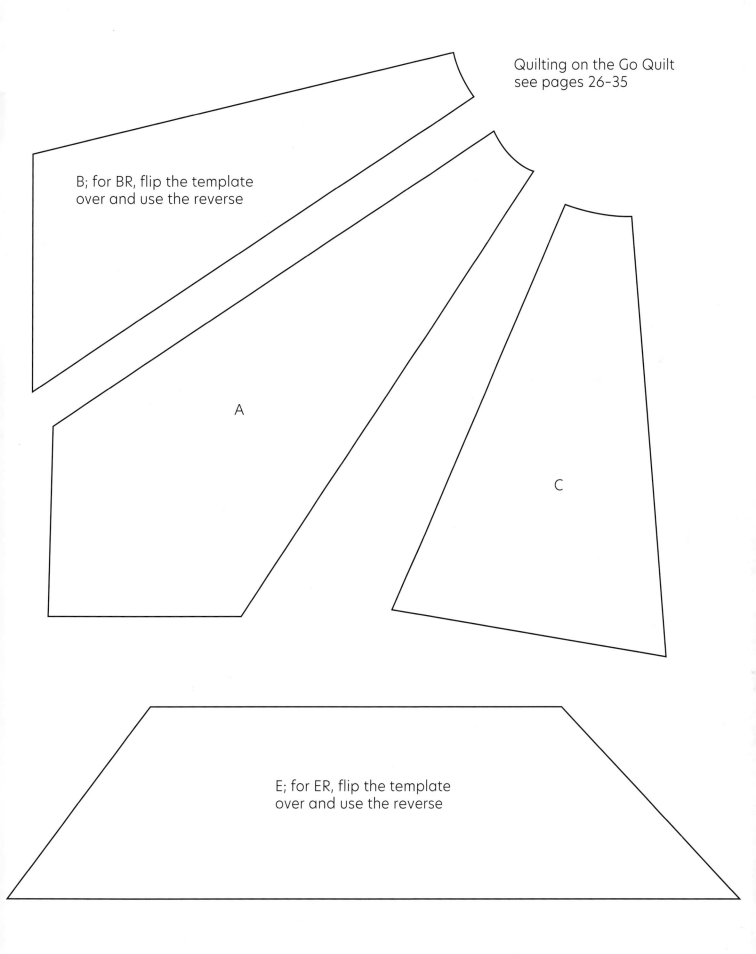

Quilting on the Go Quilt
see pages 26-35

B; for BR, flip the template
over and use the reverse

A

C

E; for ER, flip the template
over and use the reverse